THE WHITE BIKE

by Tamara von Werthern

The White Bike was first performed at The Space, London,
on 19 September 2017.

THE WHITE BIKE

by Tamara von Werthern

Cast

HENRY	**Christopher Akrill**
LILY/HANNAH/HARRIET SARAH/PC ROBERTS/ PC JONES	**Helen Millar**
DEBBIE/JULIETTE/ SALLY/PC MAXWELL	**Helen Stern**
ISABELLE	**Josephine Starte**
GUY/PAUL/SIMON	**Liam Faik**
CHILDREN'S VOICES (recorded)	**Marlene and Luka Werthern-Pilch**

Creative Team

Director	**Lily McLeish**
Designer	**Lucy Sierra**
Movement Director	**Simon Pittman**
Sound Designer	**Pete Malkin**
Lighting Designer	**Dan Saggars**
Video Designer	**Ellie Thompson**
Producer	**George Warren / Metal Rabbit Productions**
Sound Design Assistant	**Joe Dines**
Stage Manager	**Melissa Berry**
Stage Carpenter	**Jake Evans**

BIOGRAPHIES

CHRISTOPHER AKRILL (HENRY)
Christopher trained at Northern Ballet School and went on to dance at the Scottish Ballet, Northern Ballet Theatre, Malmö Ballet, Hannover Ballet and Deutsche Oper Am Rhein Dusseldorf, and Cullberg Ballet.

He is now based in London, working freelance as an actor/dancer and is co-director of HeadSpaceDance.

Theatre credits include: *The Hairy Ape* (Old Vic); *To Kill a Mockingbird* (Regent's Park/Barbican); *Lucky, Waiting for Godot* (Be Me Theatre); *Cabaret* (Lyric). He has worked with theatre directors Rufus Norris, Matthew Dunster, Timothy Sheader, Richard Jones and William Oldroyd.

Dance credits include: *Stepmother/Stepfather* (The Place); *The Odyssey* (Mark Bruce/Wilton's Music Hall); *Swan Lake, Giselle, Sleeping Beauty* (Mats Ek, Cullberg Ballet); *Romeo and Juliet* (Dusseldorf Ballet); *A Christmas Carol, Ebeneezer Scrooge* (NBT); *Sleeping Beauty, Carabos* (Hannover Staatsoper); *Pinocchio, Ghosts, Captain Alving* (ROH2); *Dr Dee* (ENO); *The Most Incredible Thing* (Sadler's Wells); *Three and Four Quarters, If Play is Play, The Canticles* (ROH2); *The Wind in the Willows, Badger* (Duchess). He has worked with choreographers Mats Ek, Jiri Kylian, Ohad Naharin, Crystal Pite, Alexander Ekman, Johan Inger, Stijn Cellis, Aletta Collins, Francesca Jaynes, Caroline Pope, Javier De Frutos, Luca Silvestrini, Mark Bruce, William Tuckett, Frantic Assembly, Scott Graham, Steven Hogget, Didy Veldman, Nils Christie, Rui Horta and Jens Östberg, Massimo Moricone, Gillian Lynne, Hans Van Manen, Nils Christie, Youri Vamos, Christopher Gable, Dennis Wayne, Nanette Glushak, Oleg Vinagradov, Quinny Sacks, Scarlett Mackmin.

Film and television credits include: *Daydreaming with Stanley Kubrick 'The Corridor'* (Black Dog Films/RSA Films; directed by Toby Dye); *Taboo* (FX miniseries; directed by Kristoffer Nyholm); *London Road* (directed by Rufus Norris); *Anna Karenina* (directed by Joe Wright); *Muppets Most Wanted* (directed by James Bobin); *Mr Selfridge* series 2 (ITV).

Choreography and movement direction credits include: *Mametz* (National Theatre Wales); *Imogen* (Shakespeare's Globe).

Awards include: Christer Holgerson's Award from the Carina Ari Memorial Foundation, and the Riksteatern Award for artistic contributions and excellence in dance.

www.headspacedance.com

HELEN MILLAR (LILY/HANNAH/HARRIET/SARAH/ PC ROBERTS/PC JONES)

Helen trained at the Drama Centre. Winner of the Alan Bates award for most outstanding newcomer. Theatre credits include: *Hamlet* (Helen was the first woman to play Hamlet in the South East of Europe); *Pygmalion* (Garrick); *Twelfth Night* (international tour); *Death and the Ploughman* (Tobacco Factory); *24 Hour Plays, Symposium, Spring, The Spies in Room 502* (The Old Vic); *21 Breaths* (Park); *Breakfast with Emma* (nominated for Best Actress in the Off West End Awards); *Surface To Air* (Arcola); *Dying* (The Gate); *Dracula: The Kisses, Peter Pan, In the Footsteps of the Mitfords, Stage Rights* (Scary Little Girls); *Macbeth* (Broadway Theatre); *Breakfast with Emma, Heartbreak House, She Stoops To Conquer, Arcadia* (Pitlochry Festival Theatre); *The Soldier's Tale, Love of the Nightingale, His Wild Imaginings* (Rough Fiction); *The Consultant, Slice* (Theatre503); *Thin Toes, The Bards of Bangkok* (Pleasance); *Love is a Smoke, Soft Armour* (Theatre Delicatessen); *Pericles, Two Gentlemen of Verona, Macbeth, The Odyssey* (Factory Theatre).

Television credits include: *Houdini & Doyle, Casualty, EastEnders, Holby City, Doctors, City Lights.* Film credits include: *Chemical Wedding, The Brink, Dark Rage, The Evening Was Long, Flash, Removed, The Rise and the Fall of the Krays, Opaque, Man of the House, Lady Macbeth.*

www.helenmillar.co.uk

HELEN STERN (DEBBIE/JULIETTE/SALLY/ PC MAXWELL)

Helen trained at Arts Educational and recently returned from eight years working in NYC.

Theatre credits include: the comedy *Lovepuke* (Gilded Balloon, Edinburgh; nominated for an Acting Excellence Award by *The Stage*); *F**king Charlie* (Tristan Bates; written and directed by Rikki Beadle-Blair); *The Francesca Woodman Project* (Martin Segal Theatre, NYC); *The Bacchae* (Actors of Dionysus tour). Helen is an audio-book narrator and has voiced over fifty titles for Audible in NYC and London. Other voice work includes playing Hela the Goddess of the Underworld in the Marvel cartoon *Thor & Loki* and narrating a documentary for Nick Hornby's charity Ministry of Stories.

NYC film credits include: *The Amazing Spider-Man 2*, and the lead in the TV movie *Control* (SyFy channel). Helen worked on the independent romantic comedy *April Flowers*, which screened at Cannes 2017. UK television credits include: *How Not to Die* (Sky One).

JOSEPHINE STARTE (ISABELLE)

Josephine graduated from the National Institute of Dramatic Art, Australia, in 2016, and from Cambridge University in 2012.

Recent credits include: *Unlocked* (AllDayBreakfast, Bristol); *The Hidden Track* (TV pilot, Russia); *I Walk In Your Words* (Rich Mix, London); *The Cherry Orchard* (New Theatre, Sydney); *Threnody* (Old Fitz, Sydney); *Trade* (HurrahHurrah, Sydney).

Winner of Best Actress, NoBudge Independent Cinema Awards, for *Blue Monday* (directed by Charles Chintzer Lai).

Josephine is also a writer and is represented by Sayle Screen.

LIAM FAIK (GUY/PAUL/SIMON)

Liam was awarded Best Actor and a first-class degree from his training on the BA acting course at Northampton University School of the Arts.

He has explored a variety of roles in both stage and screen throughout his training.

Theatre credits include: *Tape* (directed by Simon Cole); *Pornography* (directed by Dominic Rouse); *Romeo and Juliet* (directed by Emily Jenkins) and *Othello*.

Screen credits include: *Vlog Stars* (Wild Street; directed by Corry Raymond); *The Private* (directed by Maxwell Boulton in co-operation with Warner Brothers) and *Criminal Conflicts* directed by Gemma Boaden.

Liam is an active member of the National Youth Theatre of Great Britain which has helped broaden his training outside of training and offer multiple opportunities.

Liam is a very physical actor who enjoys exploring movement and storytelling through physical theatre and strives to develop this after training.

TAMARA VON WERTHERN (Playwright)

Tamara von Werthern is a playwright and producer. She studied English and Drama at Queen Mary University of London and holds an MA in Advanced Theatre Practice from Royal Central School of Speech and Drama. She is a graduate of the Royal Court Young Writers' Programme, the Almeida Theatre's WRITE Programme and has taken the Playwriting Masterclass with Stephen Jeffreys.

As a playwright, her work has been shown at the Royal Court, the Arcola Theatre, Burdall's Yard, Bath, the Lion and Unicorn Theatre, the Pleasance, Edinburgh, and Hackney Attic, as well as a number of site-specific performances with her own theatre company Para-Site Productions and Plays Rough London. Together with Lydia Fraser-Ward she founded and was co-artistic director and producer of Para-Site Productions from 2003 to 2008. She is founder and producer of Fizzy Sherbet, a writing initiative for women from across the world with regular events taking place at Hackney Attic.

Work in development includes *Jackpot*, co-written with Jack Hughes, which will receive an R&D week and rehearsed reading at the London College of Music in November 2017, also directed by Lily McLeish. Tamara has published short stories and poetry, as well as a crime novel written in German.

LILY McLEISH (Director)

Lily McLeish is a bilingual English-German theatre director. She read English literature and art history at the University of Cologne, where she worked with theatre company Port in Air. Since 2012 she has trained with Katie Mitchell and has worked as Associate Director to her on productions across Europe. She is a Creative Fellow of the RSC and Associate Director of Fizzy Sherbet.

As Director, theatre credits include: *Unlocked* (alldaybreakfast, Bristol); *A Colder Water Than Here* (VAULT); *She Echoes* (Northampton University); *Housekeeping* (LPOG, Southwark Playhouse); *Three Lives* (Fringe Arts, Bath); *Absence* (5x5x5, Young Vic); *This Despised Love* (RSC Fringe Festival); *Old Times* (Artheater, Cologne); *Footfalls* (Severins-Burg-Theater, Cologne).

As Associate Director, theatre credits include: *Anatomy of a Suicide*, *2071* (Royal Court); *Ophelias Zimmer* (Royal Court/Schaubühne, Berlin); *4.48 Psychosis*, *Reisende auf einem Bein*, *Happy Days* (Deutsches Schauspielhaus, Hamburg); *Schatten* (Schaubühne, Berlin).

As Assistant Director, theatre credits include: *Cleansed*, *The Beaux' Stratagem* (National Theatre); *The Two Gentlemen of Verona* (RSC); *The Forbidden Zone* (Salzburg Festspiele/Schaubühne, Berlin); *A Sorrow Beyond Dreams* (Burgtheater, Vienna); *The Rest Will Be Familiar to You from Cinema* (Deutsches Schauspielhaus, Hamburg); *Say It with Flowers* (Hampstead); *The Yellow Wallpaper* (Schaubühne, Berlin/Odéon Théâtre de l'Europe, Paris); *Reise durch die Nacht* (Schauspiel, Cologne/Festival d'Avignon/Theatertreffen Berlin); *Between Things* (Port in Air/Artheater, Cologne).

Awards include: Origins Award for Outstanding New Work (*A Colder Water Than Here*).

www.lilymcleish.com

LUCY SIERRA (Designer)

Recent design credits include: *Education, Education, Education* (Wardrobe Ensemble tour); *A Duckie Summer Tea Party* (Hull City of Culture); *Ode to Leeds* (West Yorkshire Playhouse); *Macbeth* (National Theatre); Young Vic 5 (Young Vic); *Cathy* (Cardboard Citizens tour); *The Grand Journey* (Bombay Sapphire Immersive Experience); *A Kid, This Tuesday* (Arcola); *The Tempest* (Royal & Derngate); *Giving* (Hampstead); *Another World* (National Theatre); *Calculating Kindness* (Camden People's Theatre); *Snow White & Rose Red* (Rash Dash/ Cambridge Arts); *Abyss* (Arcola); *Benefit, We Are All Misfits* (Cardboard Citizens tour); *We Have Fallen* (Underbelly); *If You Don't Let Us Dream, We Won't Let You Sleep* (Royal Court); *Sign of the Times* (Theatre Royal Bury); *The Bear* (Improbable tour); *Sweeney Todd, David Copperfield, White Nights* (Octagon Bolton); *Songs Inside* (Gate); *Fewer Emergencies* (Oxford Playhouse).

SIMON PITTMAN (Movement Director)

Simon is a movement director and theatre director. He is Associate Director (Learn & Train) at Frantic Assembly, Co-Director of Rough Fiction, and a selector for the National Student Drama Festival.

Movement Direction credits include: *The Box of Delights* (Wilton's Music Hall); *The Go-Between* (Apollo); *The Kingdom* (Soho); *The Curious Incident of The Dog In The Night-time* (as Associate – Gielgud); *Out of the Cage* (Park/Rose, Kingston); *The Shawshank Redemption* (Edinburgh Festival/Gaiety, Dublin); *Romeo and Juliet, The Caucasian Chalk Circle* (National Youth Theatre Wales/ Frantic Assembly); *Between Two Worlds* (Sherman, Cardiff); *Mixter Maxter, 99…100* (National Theatre of Scotland) and *365* (As associate – EIF/National Theatre of Scotland)

Directing credits include: *Othello* (National Youth Theatre of Great Britain/ Frantic Assembly/Ambassadors); *The Soldier's Tale* (Rough Fiction/London Arts Orchestra/tour); *Not a Game for Boys* (Library, Manchester); *His Wild Imaginings* (Rough Fiction at LSO St Luke's); *The Last of the Lake* (Brighton Dome/UK tour); *The Love of The Nightingale* (tour). As Associate: *The Go-Between* (West Yorkshire Playhouse); *Floyd Collins* (Southwark Playhouse); *The Shawshank Redemption* (Edinburgh Festival/Gaiety, Dublin).

Simon trained on the Birkbeck Theatre Directing MFA, as movement associate to Steven Hoggett and Scott Graham, and as resident director at The Library Theatre Manchester 2006/07.

www.simonpittman.co.uk

PETE MALKIN (Sound Designer)
As Sound Designer, theatre credits include: *The Seagull* (Lyric Hammersmith); *The Kid Stays in the Picture* (Royal Court); *Frogman* (Curious Directive); *The Tempest* (Donmar Warehouse/King's Cross); *Beware of Pity* (Schaubühne, Berlin/ Complicite); *Twelfth Night (*Manchester Royal Exchange); *Treasure* (Finborough); *Unearthed* (Arcola/UK tour); *7–75* (The Place); *Am I Dead Yet* (Unlimited/Bush); *War Correspondents* (Greenwich Festival/UK tour); *The Commission* (ROH/ Aldeburgh/Opera North); *SUN (*St Leonard's Church/ National Art Service); *Farragut North* (Southwark); *Space Junk* (Gameshow/Lyric, Hammersmith).

As co-sound designer, credits include: *The Encounter* (Complicite); *The Noise* (Northern Stage/Unlimited Theatre).

As associate sound designer, credits include: *Harry Potter and the Cursed Child* (Sonia Friedman Productions); *1984* (Headlong); *Oresteia* (West End); *Hamlet* (RSC); *Lionboy*, *The Magic Flute*, *The Master & Margarita* (Complicité).

Awards include: for Complicite's production of *The Encounter* – Special Tony Award and Drama Desk Award for Outstanding Sound Design, Evening Standard Award for Best Design, Helpmann Award for Best Sound Design.

Pete's sound work also includes co-sound designing the UN Global Goals Launch and Sydney Opera House Light the Sails events.

DAN SAGGARS (Lighting Designer)
Dan studied at Middlesex University in Lighting Design and Technical Theatre. He designs many types of performance including theatre, opera and dance. Design credits include: *How To Win Against History* (Seiriol Davies and Aine Flanagan Productions); *The Borrowers* (Polka); *Punts* (Theatre503); *Orfeo ed Euridice* (2017), *Alcina* (2016), and *Xerxes* (2015, co-design with Andy Bird) (Longborough Festival Opera); *Carry on Jaywick* (Vaults Festival/tour); Laura Lindow's *Then Leap!* (The Lowry, Manchester/rural tour); *Echo_Narcissus* (The Yard); *The Lamellar Project* (South Hill Park Studio/UK tour for Alex Marshall Design); *Vanity Fair* (Middle Temple Hall); *Only Forever* (The Hope); *The Three Musketeers* (Kenton Theatre) and *Bernarda Alba* (The Cockpit).

Upcoming projects include: *How to Win Against History* tour 2017 (Seiriol Davies and Aine Flanagan Productions).

ELLIE THOMPSON (Video Designer)
Ellie studied BATP Production Lighting at RCSSD. The course was a great way to form strong contacts for the future. Since graduating in 2014 she has collaborated with Katie Mitchell on *The Forbidden Zone* (Salzburg Festival, 2014) as Video Production Technician, and as Ingi Bekk's Associate Video Designer for *Reisende Auf Einem Bein* (Deutsches Schauspielhaus, Hamburg 2015) and *Schatten* (Schaubüehne Berlin, 2016). Further collaborations include: *The Driver's Seat* with National Theatre Scotland (Tramway, Glasgow 2015) as Video Supervisor and *The Destroyed Room* with Vanishing Point on (Scottish Tour and co-production with Battersea Arts Centre 2016) also as Video Supervisor. Most recently she has been working with National Theatre Scotland again on *Adam* as Video Supervisor during its run at the Traverse Theatre during the Edinburgh Fringe Festival 2017.

GEORGE WARREN (Producer)
George previously worked as a script-reader and developer for Scottish Screen, Nutopia, and Summit Entertainment, LA.

He founded Metal Rabbit in 2013 to pursue independent theatre projects. Recent projects include *Cargo* (Arcola); *Lardo* (Old Red Lion) and *Radiant Vermin* (Tobacco Fatory, Bristol/Soho Theatre, London/59E59, NYC). Upcoming productions include *Bookstory* (UK tour, 2017) and *Fishskin Trousers* (Park Theatre, 2017).

George was resident producer for Theatre of the Damned from 2011 to 2014, where productions included *The Horror! The Horror!* at Wilton's Music Hall (2012) and *The Ghost Hunter* at Pleasance Edinburgh and UK tour (2013). He has acted as producer for circus company Gandini Juggling since early 2015, producing their worldwide touring show *4x4: Ephemeral Architectures*.

He was a recipient of the Stage One Bursary for New Producers 2013.

JOE DINES (Sound Design Assistant)
Joe is currently studying theatre sound design at the Royal Central School of Speech and Drama. His sound designs at RCSSD include: *Maktub* (a joint production with Complicite), *Macbeth*, *Hitchcock Blonde* and *Thirteen*. His professional productions include *A Midsummer Night's Dream* as well as *Faceless* and *Virtually Related* at the Park Theatre. Joe is also a keen musician and composer.

MELISSA BERRY (Stage Manager)
Starting her career as Assistant Stage Manager on *Rotterdam* (Theatre503) in 2015, Melissa has stage-managed twenty-three shows over the last twenty-three months. After returning from Edinburgh Fringe, where she stage-managed *An Arrangement of Shoes* (The Counting House) and a two-part play *Speaking in Tongues: The Lies* and *Speaking in Tongues: The Truths* (Pleasance Courtyard), Melissa worked on *Seven Sins* (The Cockpit). Previous credits also include: *Benighted* (Old Red Lion); *My Brothers and Sisters* (Sarah Siddons Theatre); *Chummy* (White Bear) and *The View From Nowhere* (Park).

The company would like to thank:

road-peace.org.uk/donate

See Me Save Me

AUTHOR'S NOTE
Tamara von Werthern

I was cycling to work on a Monday morning. It was my first day back after my maternity leave and I had chosen a busier route than usual to minimise commuting time and have more time at home with my young daughter. By the time I came through Notting Hill I had had my fair share of close passing vehicles and near misses – and I felt a bit edgy. On the railings in the middle of the road just near to the Gate Theatre there were bunches of flowers and a photograph of a smiling thirty-year-old woman. I stopped and read the message underneath her beaming face. The woman had been killed a week earlier at that spot, crushed by a lorry. Her family were looking for witnesses to find out what had happened. Maybe it was the fact that we were the same age or that we worked in similar jobs, or even because we shared the same commute by bike, but something about her story stayed with me and made me think: What if it was me who didn't come home? The woman was Eilidh Cairns. The white bike erected in Eilidh's memory is the first permanent monument of its kind.

Following Eilidh's death, her sister, Kate, founded the campaign organisation See Me Save Me. She has been a passionate and eloquent advocate for road safety and has been taking the fight to the highest levels, including the European Parliament (and Commission). They successfully changed Directive 96/53 to enable direct-vision cabs. She also very kindly agreed to meet me, a year after Eilidh was killed, to talk about my idea of writing a play. We met several times over the years, and Kate let me see the court transcript into her sister's death, while I developed the play and tried to make it as accurate and real as possible. Her support and trust has been unwavering and I am very grateful for it.

Sadly, though, Eilidh's story is not uncommon: on average around seventeen people a year are killed on London's roads alone.* There are no comprehensive records for the whole of the UK, or worldwide, but this is clearly an indication of the scale of the problem. In the last year alone, three extremely experienced long-distance cycle racers have been killed; one of them, Mike Hall, was the founder of the TransContinental Cycle Race. He was thirty-five.

I feel that this is an important story to be told – one that affects all of us as road users of whichever kind – and I would love the play to help spread the message around the world. As Kate Cairns says: 'Art is a force for change, and we do hope to change the perception of these deaths. It is easy to brush them aside, blame the cyclist for not wearing a helmet, notice the statistics but forget the human story behind the numbers.'

This is one such story – there are many more out there. I hope this play can be another kind of memorial.

* Average between 1986–2010; source: cyclingintelligence.com

PRODUCTION NOTE

The White Bike is set along an existing route in Hackney, East London. I made this choice because I thought it was important that people watching the play – at The Space on the Isle of Dogs, also in East London – could relate to events taking place in the real world around where they lived. In future productions of the play, I am very happy for the route to be changed to reflect the local area, in order to achieve the same effect.

Part of the cycling experience is that the places you pass by and through all spark images and ideas in your mind, so it is important when making changes that Isabelle's memories and flashbacks are a direct result of what she sees around her. When cycling, your mind works differently – many long-distance cyclists have said, for example, that the greatest challenge when riding for days is not the physical exhaustion, but being alone with your thoughts.

Showing cycling on stage is a particular challenge. For the original production at The Space, director Lily McLeish and I knew that we wanted to translate the experience of cycling onto the stage. So instead of simply seeing a woman on a bicycle we focused on creating a physical movement piece with bike parts. We found a stage language that allowed fluid movement between the journey on the bicycle and the memories.

However, the play is written so that other staging solutions for the cycling are possible, even encouraged. There are various ways in which Isabelle's journey can be shown on stage. You could use video recordings of the route. There could be a map projected at the back, maybe with a moving dot. A bike could be suspended in the air. Or fixed to the floor so that it remains stationary when pedalled. The play could even be staged outside of a theatre, site-specifically, on an actual journey with an actual bike…

The number of actors in the cast is also flexible. It can be performed with a cast of three, in a simple setting, or a full cast of fourteen. You could cast Isabelle with two actors, one to play her 'physical' self and one to speak her thoughts aloud. You could cast a child as Lily. Alternatively, you could record Isabelle's thoughts – and the child's voice at the end. There are many different staging options, and you are welcome to try them.

When producing the play at The Space, we also offered workshops for Hackney Council and Discover Young Hackney Festival and to local schools. The workshop was called 'Staging the Impossible' and explored how to find solutions for seemingly impossible stage directions by using your imagination. I like to think that this is a play that requires just this sort of approach.

EILIDH CAIRNS
12th June 1978–5th February 2009

Eilidh Jake Cairns grew up on the Northumberland coast, the youngest of four siblings. She loved the ocean, mountains and desert and crawled with delight into the waves for the first time before she could even walk. She studied Marine Biology at Liverpool John Moores University, learning about the depths beneath the sea. After graduating she followed her passion for the outdoors, spending three seasons in the Alps where she mastered snowboarding and made masses of friends.

Afterwards she went to Dubai to work on wildlife documentaries, focusing on the rich marine life of the Gulf. Moving to London, Eilidh replicated the outdoor feeling of freedom and independence by going everywhere on her bike. She worked up the career ladder and had just found her 'dream job' making documentaries for Smithson.

Her wit, charm and empathy meant she was at the centre of a big group of many who felt as close to her as a sister. When she died, she was living with friends near Hampstead Heath and was very happy with her boyfriend Giles.

Eilidh died on the 5th February 2009 after being hit from behind by a fully laden tipper truck. The driver said he did not see her. She had left her home at Kingswear Road, near Hampstead Heath, and cycled her usual ten-mile route to Chiswick. She had been cycling this route for over two years, and was a fit and experienced cyclist, well aware of the dangers of HGVs. Eilidh was struck at 8.56 a.m., just as she approached a pedestrian crossing in Notting Hill Gate. She lay pinned by the wheels, fully conscious, and asking passers-by to 'Please help me, please help me'. Low cloud on the day prevented the air ambulance reaching her, and Eilidh was eventually taken by ambulance to the Royal London Hospital, where, despite the best endeavours of a team of trauma specialists, she died at 10.48 a.m.

The driver was eventually found to have defective vision but there was no charge in relation to Eilidh's death, and he was allowed to continue driving his truck. Fifteen months later he ran down and killed ninety-seven-year-old Holocaust survivor Nora Gutmann on a pedestrian crossing.

The White Bike is written in memory of Eilidh, and the many other cyclists who have been killed on the roads of London. For more information, visit **www.eilidhcairns.com**

See Me Save Me

Across the UK and further afield, too many people are killed or seriously injured every year in collisions with heavy goods vehicles (HGVs) – and most of those collisions could be prevented.

HGVs are disproportionately represented in cyclists' fatalities, with 50% of deaths involving an HGV even though such vehicles make up only 4% of traffic. Construction vehicles are most prevalent in crashes because cement mixers, tipper lorries and skip lorries are designed with massive blind areas all around the cab. Drivers consistently say they did not see the victim, and legislation to increase mirrors on vehicles has not solved the problem.

- This is not just a cyclists' issue. Twice as many pedestrians are killed by HGVs than cyclists.

- This is not just a London issue. There are many more victims across the UK than in London.

- This is not just an urban issue. Mile for mile, the risk of death on rural roads is around 1.7 times that on urban roads.

These collisions ruin lives – for the killed or injured, for the drivers of the HGV, for the witnesses, for the families, friends and colleagues of everyone involved.

See Me Save Me works to eradicate collisions between HGVs and more vulnerable road users. We want a society where everyone is able to use our streets, whatever their chosen mode of transport, without risk or fear of death or injury through a collision.

You can take action by:

- Donating
- Signing up to our emails
- Writing to your MP
- Writing to your local authority to demand responsible procurement
- Reporting bad driving
- Volunteering time and expertise (fundraising, PR, social media)
- Suggesting your company supports our campaign
- Spreading the word (follow us on Twitter: @SeeMeSaveMe)

For more information, visit **www.seemesaveme.org**

THE WHITE BIKE

Tamara von Werthern

The White Bike was first performed in an earlier version at the Arcola Theatre, London, as part of the Made in Hackney Festival, in July 2010, with the following cast:

ISABELLE   Lois Jones
HENRY   Jack Hughes
DEBBIE   Rosalind Philips

Director   Caroline Leslie

Acknowledgements

Thank you to everyone who helped bring this play to the stage.
Lily McLeish, so glad to have found you. Thank you to
Christopher Akrill, Helen Millar, Helen Stern, Josephine Starte,
Liam Faik, Lucy Sierra, Simon Pittman, Pete Malkin, Dan
Saggars, Ellie Thompson, Melissa Berry, Joe Dines and George
Warren – you were a dream to work with. Thank you to all our
supporters on Kickstarter and our individual donors. Thank you to
all the actors who were so crucial in the development of the play:
Lois Jones, Rosalind Philips, Jack Hughes, Caroline Pegg, Kellie
Higgins, Jot Davies, Chris Harper, Martin Bassindale, Daphne
Alexander, Claire Lams, Thomas Brownlee and Mark Conway.
Thank you to directors Caroline Leslie and Oliver Rose. Thank
you to Sandra Buch, Duncan Macmillan and the Arcola Theatre
Writers Group. Thank you to Kim Harding at EdFoC, Jules
Deering at QMUL, Steph Weller, Joanne Black, Claas Mehlkopp,
Lilli Geissendorfer at the Almeida, Louise Stephens at the Royal
Court, Donnachadh McCarthy from StopKillingCyclists and
Amanda Whittington. Thank you to Nick Hern, Matt Applewhite,
Sarah Liisa Wilkinson, Jodi Gray, Jon Barton, Robin Booth, Ian
Higham, Siân Mayhall-Purvis, Tim Digby-Bell, Marcelos Dos
Santos and John O'Donovan. Thank you to Debbie Dorling for
speaking with me about her experience. A big thank you to Kate
Cairns who shared her story with me and supported the project all
the way. Thank you to my mum Julia, who came to see all
versions of this play, and all my extended family on both sides
(Werthern & Pilch). Thank you James, Marlene and Luka –
you're the best and I couldn't have done it without you.

T.v.W.

For Marlene

Characters

ISABELLE
HENRY, *her husband*
LILY, *her daughter, approaching her first birthday, and at six*
HANNAH, *a local mum*
GUY, *a van driver*
DEBBIE, *a witness*
JULIETTE, *Isabelle's mum*
SIMON
SARAH
SALLY
HARRIET, *a midwife*
PAUL, *a lorry driver*
POLICE OFFICER ROBERTS, *female*
POLICE OFFICER MAXWELL, *female*
POLICE OFFICER JONES, *female*

This text went to press before the end of rehearsals and so may differ slightly from the play as performed.

6.30 a.m. Tuesday 21st October 2008.

It's dark. An alarm bell rings. And rings. And rings.

ISABELLE. Henry.

HENRY!

Turn it off.

HENRY. Hmmm?

ISABELLE. Turn. It. Off.

HENRY. Hmmm?

The light flicks on and ISABELLE *stretches over* HENRY's *prostrate body to turn off the alarm.*

ISABELLE. Jesus Christ.

She sits up in bed but is in no way awake, her hair is a mess and she can barely open her eyes.

For fuck's sake.

Why is it so loud?

Henry? Why do you –

There's no point – he's asleep.

I need some coffee.

A young child starts crying in the other room.

Ah, no! See what you've done?

I'm here, I'm coming, darling!

I could have done with a shower, I'll get you back for this…

6.55 a.m. Tuesday 21st October 2008. ISABELLE *enters fully dressed in office clothes, with a steaming cafetière, two mugs, and carrying* LILY – *also dressed, with a fresh nappy etc. – a muslin cloth slung over her shoulder.*

Are you still asleep?

She pours the coffees. HENRY *sits up in bed.*

I had to change the sheets. The nappy leaked again. Can you try and get some new covers? You could go over to Clissold Park if you're going to Stoke Newington anyway?

ISABELLE *sits next to him in bed, sips coffee and cuddles with* LILY.

(*To* LILY.) You smell so good. Just here. Yes you do. Now that you're clean. (*To* HENRY.) I've fed her as well. (*To* LILY.) Does that tickle?

HENRY. You're Wonder Woman.

ISABELLE. I know. (*To* LILY.) Are you going to the park with Daddy? On the massive big slide? Yep. Yes, you are. (*To* HENRY.) Get the ones with the poppers, okay? They're better.

7.35 a.m. Tuesday 21st October 2008.

The toaster pops out two pieces of toast. ISABELLE *and* HENRY *sit next to each other with the* Guardian Weekend *spread all over the table. They spread butter and marmalade on the toast and eat, while reading. Radio 4 in the background.* LILY *is now asleep in a sling on* HENRY, *who is dressed casually in dad-at-home clothes. Companionable silence.*

She asleep?

HENRY. Think so.

ISABELLE. I'm jealous.

HENRY. Yeah.

ISABELLE. I was up twice. Just keep nodding off while she drinks.

HENRY. I'm sorry. I tried to, you know, let you have some sleep, but there's only so much walking up and down a corridor one man can do.

ISABELLE. I know. Don't worry, I'll be fine.

HENRY. Coffee saves lives.

ISABELLE. Exactly.

ISABELLE folds the paper and gets up.

Okay, I'm off then.

HENRY. Have a good day.

ISABELLE. You too. And don't forget the covers, okay?

HENRY. Yeah, sure.

ISABELLE. Ah, the romance.

HENRY. Come here, I'll give you romance.

They kiss.

ISABELLE. Bye, you.

And you.

She kisses the swaddled top of LILY's head through the cover of the sling and leaves.

7.52 a.m. Tuesday 21st October 2008. ISABELLE cycles. There's a blue sky and sun, but it is cold.

(*Direct address/thought.*) Shame she's asleep, I love her waving at the window. Little fat hands. Love those hands.

Brrr, winter soon, hate having to cycle back in the dark. Summer's so much better.

The sound of a motorcycle going past, the image of broken double yellow lines as she's cycling along.

Summer smells of leather and petrol. Sand everywhere, in your socks, between your teeth, in all the sandwiches... My dad with full hair and how broad his back was! I hold on tight, lean into the turnings, same as him. Anna is in the side-car – the yellow helmet catching the sun. 'Do you want to fly?' He turns the corner and the side-car flies up in the air like a carousel pod.

Squeals of delight.

She stops at a pedestrian crossing. A woman with a pushchair is crossing. It's HANNAH from NCT.

HANNAH. You back at work already?

ISABELLE. Yes, nearly three weeks now...

HANNAH. That's flown by, hasn't it?

ISABELLE. Tell me about it – whoosh and it's gone. I miss spending my mornings in the café. How long have you got left?

HANNAH. Until January. I took the whole year in the end.

ISABELLE. Oh, lucky you!

HANNAH. I'll have forgotten everything when I get back! Anyway, best get on. You have a good day.

ISABELLE. Thanks! Let's grab a coffee soon, okay?

HANNAH. Great. Let's catch up properly. With the kids. I'll text you.

7.58 a.m. Tuesday 21st October 2008. ISABELLE cycles on, up a little hill, along a busy road with heavy traffic. She turns right, the road is flat now, and quieter. She gets faster, gets into rhythm of cycling, breathes.

ISABELLE (*direct address/thought*). My fingers are freezing, maybe Primark is open already? They're evil though, child labour, ah well, they're cheap, cheap gloves.

The beeping and clanking of a refuse-collection vehicle, as she overtakes it. It smells. A lot.

Hope Henry put the bin out. We need to get more bin bags. And recycling bags... Washing-up liquid. Even my ears are getting cold now. Red. I can feel the red creeping up.

8.09 a.m. Tuesday 21st October 2008. ISABELLE is now going along Dalston Lane, other cyclists have joined her and they are negotiating the traffic and each other. A car honks its horn.

What's the hurry? You're too fast anyway. There's a school over there. That's probably it, actually – Chelsea-tractor brat drop-off.

Snatches of radio hang in the air – the cyclists are faster than the cars. A lot of tailback. A car is parked in the cyclist's advance box. The cyclists queue on the left-hand side next to the traffic, as the box is blocked.

Of course he'll nudge into the advance box. I knew it. Every bloody time.

8.13 a.m. Tuesday 21st October 2008. The lights change, ISABELLE *turns left into Kingsland Road. The Tesco Metro has started putting up Christmas decorations.*

Christmas lights in the trees already! Pretty. Mums with buggies – that's me now as well... I've joined the buggy parade. December soon. Lily's first Christmas. Must make an advent calendar.

Breath.

That'll be fun. Little things. Crayons. Bath toys.

Breath.

We'll hang it up over her bed, on a washing line.

8.20 a.m. Tuesday 21st October 2008. ISABELLE *is waiting at another set of lights. A* GUY *leans out of the passenger seat of a van.*

GUY. Nice titties!

ISABELLE *stares straight ahead, pretending not to have heard him.*

ISABELLE (*direct address/thought*). Fuck you.

GUY. Oi! Didn't ya hear me? I said 'nice tits!'

ISABELLE (*direct address/thought*). What do you think, you asshole? If I could, I'd kick you so hard in the balls that you couldn't sit for weeks.

8.22 a.m. Tuesday 21st October 2008. ISABELLE *cycles on.* GUY *honks the horn of the van appreciatively while driving off.*

What gives you the right to talk to me like that? Do you think it turns women on? You small-pricked excuse for a man. Stupid... stupid... As soon as I'm online you go straight onto Everyday Sexism, you prick. Stupid little... ah, I'm not even going to waste my breath on you. Fuck, it's freezing!

Breath.

We should have a proper winter holiday this year. Show Lily some snow. Soft snow, freezing air. Not like the grey slush you get here. Take my board. Blue skies and soft white snow, wrapping the mountain, making everything rounded and padded and safe. Just me and the speed of the board, everything goes quiet and moves away from me, the board slices through the snow, glides over it. Leaning into the turns, spraying snow behind me.

8.29 a.m. Tuesday 21st October 2008. ISABELLE *approaches the Oxfam shop on Kingsland Road.*

Oxfam! Must look for a coat in here. I love the way the city looms up at the end of the road like some fairytale land – *Wizard of Oz.* Brrr. Can't even feel my fingers any more. LPs hanging from the ceiling… a mannequin getting dressed… I love this shop. Let's have a look at the weekend.

8.30 a.m. Tuesday 21st October 2008.

A lorry overtakes her and turns left. She narrowly avoids being crushed under its wheels. The sickening sound of brakes screaming and the lorry grinding to a halt. DEBBIE *has seen everything and puts both hands in front of her mouth. There is a slight time-wobble here, and the light changes, maybe just for a moment.*

(*To lorry.*) Watch out! You idiot! Charging round the corner like that. You could have killed me!

(*Direct address/thought.*) Bloody hell. You need nerves of steel. Phew…

She starts humming. Then starts singing 'Don't Stop Me Now' by Queen, loud, enthusiastically, knowing that it's all swallowed up by the traffic anyway.

Love singing on the bike. People do it all the time! Catch these snatches when you're cycling past, sometimes even opera. Best thing about being on the bike, you're in your own world.

She slows down a bit, and cycles on, but more gently.

And at night, long after the rush hour, when it's quiet. When there's been rain and the streets are slick with lights. Bright-yellow windows and glimpses of other lives. Bookshelves reaching up to the ceiling. Someone smoking out of an open window.

That's when I feel I'm a part of London.

ISABELLE *stops at a red light.*

Red car. Blue van. Massive Uber-taxi. Long-haired male driver. Little old lady driver. All spinning round this corner as I'm waiting for a green light.

8.46 a.m. Tuesday 21st October 2008. SARAH *is sidling up on her bike next to* ISABELLE. *She looks at her funny, really stares at her.* ISABELLE *feels uncomfortable.*

SARAH. You're new here?

ISABELLE. What?

SARAH. Haven't seen you around.

ISABELLE. Yes, so?

SARAH. Oh, okay. Well, have a good day.

ISABELLE (*weirded out*). Okay?

ISABELLE *cycles off as the traffic starts moving around her.* SARAH *fades into the background. The sound of a lorry thundering past.* ISABELLE *shudders.*

Better get off the main road.

She indicates and turns left. A crow is cawing. The sound of water lapping against stone. The traffic sounds are now very distant.

(*Direct address/thought.*) Ahhh. The canal. It's like being in the countryside. Birds swooping. The little waves rippling the surface of the water. A Christmas tree on a house boat!

She breathes in a big mouthful of air. There's a ting ting ting as another bike goes under a bridge.

I'd love to live on a houseboat. It looks so pretty, all the different colours, blue, green, red. Lily would enjoy seeing ducks out of the window. It must be nice to feel the movement of the water. And it's so peaceful here. Nettles on the side. Woodsmoke from a boat chimney. Flowerpots on the roof. That's a good life. I love the tiny rowing boat tied to the bigger boat there, like a mother and child. 'Darling, can you row down to the market to get some croissants, I'll make coffee – and don't forget the paper!' And then you sit on your tiny metal porch, or on the roof, and let the day unfold. The whisks and cooking spoons hanging up by the window!

Pause. ISABELLE is enjoying the sun on her face, the wind in her hair.

When I'm on the Tube, I never really look at things.

Nobody does, do they? Some people are watching films on their tablets, or reading, or just staring straight ahead trying to avoid anyone's eye. Or playing Candy Crush.

And the ads are all about orphans or cancer.

No air. No room.

But here… you can breathe. There's a paper cup floating on the water. A plane overhead. The world is just so much more open. Bricks. Graffiti. A crumpled beer can under a tree.

8.51 a.m. Tuesday 21st October 2008. ISABELLE rings her bell, then turns left. Up a little hill. She is now in Broadway Market, a small road off the canal, lined with cafés and little shops. She stops at Sultan Organic Food Grocery & Wine, the corner shop just by London Fields. She leans the bike against a pole and looks at the fruit and vegetables on display.

Asparagus, artichokes, apricots… ah. Avocado. Lily's favourite. Mashed up with banana – gross, but Lily loves it.

For me it was apple. My mum would grate it on an orange plastic grater, and feed me with a plastic spoon, amazing that I can remember that grater. I must have been tiny.

12.35 a.m. Wednesday 12th July 1980, the South of France.

JULIETTE. Open wide! Here comes the choo-choo train…

ISABELLE swallows a spoonful, smiles.

Good girl!

She touches one of the avocado pears to test it. Is confused. Touches another one. There is something wrong, and she

*can't feel the avocado pears, but she does not want to
acknowledge it to herself. She looks at her hands, lost.*

ISABELLE. They have to be ripe. I'm not going to bother with
these. I have to squash them, or it won't work.

ISABELLE *gets her bike and pushes it to the pedestrian
crossing and across. She's in the park. It is May 1984.*

JULIETTE. Okay, on you get. Don't be scared, I'm holding it
steady, see?

ISABELLE. Don't let go, *Maman*, okay?

JULIETTE. I won't.

ISABELLE *climbs onto the bike, full of respect for the beast,
her feet angling for the pedals.*

Well done. Now put your feet on the pedals – good. And push.

ISABELLE. But don't let go!

JULIETTE. I won't, I promise.

JULIETTE *holds on to the bike frame and runs with the bike
while* ISABELLE *cycles, getting steadier as she goes.
Eventually* JULIETTE *lets go, but still runs with the bike,
then falls behind.*

ISABELLE. *Maman?* Are you still holding on?

JULIETTE. You're doing it! You're cycling. Look straight
ahead, keep pedalling. Very good!

ISABELLE. I am? Oh yes. Look!

JULIETTE. Beautiful! Well done!

ISABELLE. I'm cycling! I'm cycling really fast! *Maman*, look!
I'm really fast!

JULIETTE. Careful now, not too…

ISABELLE *starts wobbling, then falls spectacularly off the
bike. She starts bawling.*

That's okay, darling, up you get! You're fine.

ISABELLE (*wails loudly*). *Maman!*

JULIETTE *wraps her up in her arms and shushes her.*

JULIETTE. There there, it's okay, darling. Bend your leg? See, it still works.

ISABELLE. There's blood! *Maman*, I'm bleeding!

JULIETTE. Just a scratch. We'll put a plaster on at home.

ISABELLE. But it hurts!

JULIETTE. I know. You are very brave. Do you want to have another go now?

ISABELLE *nods, wipes at her eyes.*

Good girl. Come on, get straight back in the saddle. That's it.

JULIETTE *helps her into the saddle, gives her a push and watches her cycle off, now grown up again.*

8.57 a.m. Tuesday 21st October 2008. ISABELLE *is cycling through the park. The sound of leaves rustling and her wheel going through puddles.*

ISABELLE (*direct address/thought*). Golden yellow leaves. Dark red. Three dogs running off the leash. A man with earphones on top of his red woollen hat. A woman walking with a big paper bag, smoking. A bush with red berries waving at me.

My little private bike road.

Amazing light, so intense – maybe there'll be a storm later.

Solid black clouds massing up.

Hackney Picture House... The big letters made from metal netting. Lights in the trees outside. I remember when that was Ocean. When I was younger, we would go out here nearly every weekend.

8.08 p.m. Saturday 14th May 1995. ISABELLE *is at home, a teenager. She is about to leave the house,* JULIETTE *intercepts her at the door.*

JULIETTE. Are you off, Chouchou?

ISABELLE. Yeah, bye, Mum!

JULIETTE. Now remember what I said about sex.

ISABELLE. Mum!

JULIETTE. Have you got condoms in your bag?

ISABELLE. You are so embarrassing – I'm not... going to have sex. I'm fifteen! I'm not even legal.

JULIETTE. Well, you never know.

ISABELLE. Mum, you can trust me on that.

JULIETTE. I'm just saying it's always good to be prepared. Nothing wrong with sex, it's good to talk about it.

ISABELLE. You talk about it way too much!

JULIETTE. Better than too little. You know you can always – Hang on – that's my scarf – isn't that my scarf?

ISABELLE. You'll get it back, don't worry.

JULIETTE. Well, it suits you better than me. You look beautiful. Keep it. How are you getting home?

ISABELLE. I don't know, it's not far, we'll walk.

JULIETTE. I don't want you walking on your own when it's late. Ring me, I'll pick you up. I can drop Ellie too.

ISABELLE. Okay, thanks, Mum. Love you. Bye.

JULIETTE. Bye, my love. See you later. And remember what I said –

ISABELLE. Yeah yeah. I have to go now, bye, Mum!

1995–2005. Suddenly there is dry ice and flashing disco lights, loud pop music, ISABELLE *is dancing together with the others, at first self-conscious and aware of being looked at, then more and more uninhibited, she's dancing as if nobody is watching. The music changes to show how time and her taste is changing, and the lighting becomes more 'cellar bar' than 'big club venue'.*

(*Direct address/thought, overlapping the dance sequence.*)
I love going out. Love dancing. Always have. The coloured lights... the smoke in the air... feeling your body move in this sea of other bodies... when the music shakes your bones and moves you from inside and you just feel... alive.

Ellie and me would get drunk on two bottles of beer, hide in the toilets to talk about boys and write on the walls. And dance and dance. After Ocean, there were other places, little cellar bars that sprung up along Kingsland Road and Old Street. I had my first joint by the bins behind Trash, my first kiss next to the toilets at The Old Blue Last, and my first break-up in the smoky bar of The Shacklewell Arms.

9.03 p.m. Saturday 6th August 2005. ISABELLE *arrives outside a gig, realises she doesn't have her bike lock with her.* HENRY *is just locking up his bike.*

Sorry, excuse me?

HENRY. Yeah?

ISABELLE. Is that your bike?

HENRY. No, I'm nicking it.

ISABELLE. Oh. Okay. Sorry.

HENRY. I was joking – haven't got my tools with me tonight.

ISABELLE. Ah. Ha ha. Funny.

HENRY. Why do you ask?

ISABELLE. Oh, I've been really stupid, I forgot to take my lock.

HENRY. Ah, no. Bad luck.

ISABELLE. So. Are you here for the gig?

HENRY. Yeah, why?

ISABELLE. So could I maybe lock my bike up with yours?

HENRY. Oh. Yeah, sure. Why not? Good idea.

ISABELLE. So stupid, leaving the house without a lock.

HENRY. It's not a problem. This is big enough for two.

ISABELLE. Thanks. Well, I guess I'll see you after then.

HENRY. How will I find you? Could get busy.

ISABELLE. Oh, yes.

HENRY. I can't just leave your bike here and cycle off, can I?

ISABELLE. No, that would be extremely rude. Can we swap numbers?

HENRY. Great. Let's. I'm Henry, by the way.

ISABELLE. Isabelle.

HENRY. Nice to meet you.

ISABELLE. You too. (*Types into phone.*) Henry.

9.02 a.m. Tuesday 21st October 2008.

ISABELLE *is back on the bike, now cycling past the town hall.*

(*Direct address/thought.*) We got married here. On a Tuesday afternoon, just the two of us. Hackney Town Hall with flags on top. The big clock, steps leading up. We asked a woman to take a picture of us on the steps here – must be in a drawer somewhere. I wore a dark-blue dress. I need to put that album together, I really do.

And we registered Lily's birth here… she was so tiny then. With her monk's hair. Awww. Three weeks maybe? It's not as nice looking on the inside, all brown corridors and plastic floors.

So many grand-looking houses like that. Probably all divided into a squillion flats and bedsits. London is so expensive. Everyone squished together.

There is a sudden rumble of thunder.

Ah, no! Hope it won't rain. I hate cycling through the rain.

Wet jeans clinging to your thighs… rain driving in your face… water dripping from the back of your helmet down your neck.

A bus passes and ISABELLE *coughs.*

You can SMELL the pollution in the air. There's no getting away from it. Toxic.

We need to move away really. Get some fresh air. But then, what's the point?

The whole world is going to shit.

I'm terrified about climate change. I lie awake at night sometimes, worrying about what the world will be like when Lily is my age. If there'll be wars over food, and a tsunami breaking over the Thames Barrier. If life will be really hard for her.

She indicates to turn right and moves over into the middle of the road. This is a tricky turning, as you can't properly see around the bend of the road, and as she turns, she is distracted by seeing SALLY *asleep on the pavement. A car whooshes past and she wobbles and nearly comes off the bike.*

(*To bike.*) Idiot! Watch what you're doing – *connard*! They charge around that corner like nobody's business.

(*Direct address/thought – deep breath in.*) That woman under the railway bridge. She's completely exposed there, sprawled on the pavement. Why is everyone walking so close to her? Everyone looks at their bloody phones, huddled into their scarves. She's in summer clothes. She must be freezing.

(*Addressing passers-by.*) Excuse me… Sorry, do you see that woman over there? Do you think we should… ehm, hello!?

(*Direct address/thought.*) Rude! They didn't even break their step!

Why are people so rude? I hate it.

(*To* SALLY.) Hello? Do you need anything? Do you need some money?

SALLY (*sleepy*). What?

ISABELLE. Can I give you some money?

SALLY. Money? What's that gonna do?

ISABELLE. Or a cup of tea, or… You must be freezing.

SALLY. I'm alright, love. You take care now, watch how you go.

ISABELLE. Um. Thanks. Are you sure…?

SALLY. I'm fine. How old are you?

ISABELLE. Um, twenty-nine.

SALLY. That's a crying shame.

ISABELLE. Oh. Okay. I'd best be off.

SALLY. Too bloody young.

ISABELLE. Bye then.

She's back on her bike.

Let's go through the graveyard here.

5.45 p.m. Monday 21st May 2007. ISABELLE *jumps off the bike and leans it against a tree. She is waiting for* HENRY. *He arrives with a small bunch of flowers, clearly freshly picked from a nearby flowerbed. She jumps up at him and wraps her legs round him.*

Hey.

HENRY. Ooh. You're light as a feather.

He puts her down.

ISABELLE. Are these for me?

HENRY. No. For my other girlfriend.

ISABELLE *pushes him away forcefully in total outrage.*

Ouch – that's actually quite painful.

ISABELLE. Yep. Don't mess with me.

HENRY. Is it the hormones? Will I be physically abused for the next half-year?

ISABELLE. Probably.

HENRY. Ah well, as long as I know where I'm at.

ISABELLE. Okay, give them here then. You did just nick them over there, didn't you?

HENRY. It's the thought that counts.

ISABELLE. Oh yeah.

She kisses him, then hooks her arm under his, they start walking.

HENRY. How's the little peanut? Have you been looking after her?

ISABELLE. How do you know we're having a girl?

HENRY. I just know.

ISABELLE. Really? That's my job, 'to know'... oh why don't we find out?

HENRY. No way. Where's the fun in that?

ISABELLE. But I can't wait! And we'll need to agree on two names, that's impossible. You haven't even agreed to one of the ones I like.

HENRY. I like Lily.

ISABELLE. Okay. You do? And if it's a boy?

HENRY. Theodoreus.

ISABELLE. You're an idiot! (*Pushes him again.*)

HENRY. Ouch! You're dangerous!

> *9.07 a.m. Tuesday 21st October 2008.* ISABELLE *is on the bike again, now cycling through the City Academy, towards Homerton Hospital.*

ISABELLE (*direct address/thought*). Big square... tombstones like fridges... pigeons... the white tower of St John's. Next to the graveyard is the walled-garden playground behind heavy iron gates painted teal, it's usually full of picnic blankets and screaming toddlers but now it's washed clean by the rain. Puddles everywhere.

> *There is a moment where* ISABELLE *realises that it is raining – she hasn't noticed before, because she can't feel the rain on her skin. A small moment where she takes this in, then shakes off the oddness of it.*

It's warm.

> *She cycles from the quiet of the graveyard and playground, where we can hear her go through puddles, onto a busy road. She crosses it and continues onto the pavement and through a walkway by a school.*

Little short cut through City Academy... the big glass window into the dining hall... turquoise walls... menus on tables... bowls with green apples... uniformed kids at breakfast club...

Much faster, this way. A white bike painted on the ground.

When we moved, it took nearly an hour in the van – the same distance that takes ten minutes on a bike. No wonder there's all this road rage. Most drivers hate cyclists simply because they're faster than them. So of course they feel terribly insulted if a cyclist whizzes past them when they're stuck in traffic. It takes so little to make them explode. I read about a guy in a car running down a cyclist *on the pavement*. He got so angry at being confronted by him for cutting him off, he actually mounted the pavement and ran him down.

Ah, there's the hospital. Ambulances, green and yellow… man on crutches… vehicle reversing. Beep beep beep. The glass doors sliding open, like a mouth waiting to swallow you up.

14th March 2007. ISABELLE *is in labour,* HENRY *kneeling behind her, supporting her. In the background, 'Sugar Man' by Rodriguez is playing from a playlist. The atmosphere is calm and relaxed, the two work as a team and concentrate on the task in hand. When there is a contraction,* ISABELLE'*s breathing changes and becomes deep and focused – apart from this there is no sign of pain, or even discomfort.* HENRY *gently strokes her arm during the contractions, they don't need to talk about what they are doing.*

HENRY. Water?

ISABELLE. Yes, please.

She drinks from a bottle. He wipes her forehead with a damp cloth.

HENRY. You okay?

ISABELLE. Yeah, it's completely gone in between.

HENRY. Do you need anything else?

ISABELLE. Hang on… here it comes.

Contraction. Calm. She breathes, he strokes her arm.

HENRY. You're doing so well. I'm really proud of you.

ISABELLE. Thanks. Can't believe it's really happening.

HENRY. Yes, and you're so good at it!

ISABELLE. Who would have thought, eh?

They laugh.

HARRIET, *the midwife, comes in to check on them.*

HARRIET. Still having fun then? That's good.

She checks ISABELLE*'s blood pressure with a strap and a pump and looks at the monitor while she does so.*

Okay, how's the monitor? Heartbeat is stable so far.

Deflates the pressure, looks at the result.

Ah. Your BP is a bit high, let me get you something to keep it down. Let's just check the cervix now.

HENRY. Sorry, but we said no drugs if possible…

HARRIET. Okay, not much progress there, but that's okay – four centimetres.

An alarm sounds from another room.

Right, just keep doing what you're doing, it all looks fine so far, I'll be back, okay?

HENRY. Could we get some more water, please? And maybe ice?

HARRIET. Yes, I'll tell the nurse. Sorry, I have to run. Lots of emergencies today.

HENRY. God, they're busy. I wouldn't want to work for the NHS. Hectic out there, isn't it?

ISABELLE (*makes a distracted sound of agreement*). Mh.

HENRY. Still, it's nice we got Harriet again. She's good, isn't she?

ISABELLE. Henry…

HENRY. Yes? What?

ISABELLE. I feel a bit funny…

HENRY. What do you mean?

ISABELLE. Bit floaty, bit sick.

HENRY. I'll go and get…

ISABELLE. No, stay, please… Arrrgh –

Another contraction, this time louder and more painful, with HENRY *looking on, helpless.*

HENRY. I'm right here, it's okay, it'll be fine.

Suddenly the same alarm rings out from right next to them.

ISABELLE. What is that? What does it mean? Henry, what should we do?

HENRY *(runs to the door and shouts).* Hello! Hello, we need some help here. Please can someone come?

HARRIET *hurries back in, takes one look at the monitor, and starts talking into her walkie-talkie.*

HARRIET. Room 356. Baby in distress, please send anaesthetist and obstetrician through, preparing for emergency C-section.

HARRIET *brings a form to* ISABELLE *and holds out a pen.*

Right, darling, I'm so sorry, but we need to get this baby out and fast, so we're going to bring you into the theatre now. We need to hurry a bit, so we'll explain what we're doing along the way, but first I need you to sign this. It's a very safe operation, but there is a small risk to both you and the baby, so we need you to agree with it, so please could you just sign here.

HENRY. Sign for what?

HARRIET. Well, in case of death of either mother or infant. We are going to try and save her life before your baby's life, because the two of you can have more children, after all. It used to be the other way round, but they've changed it. Mother before baby. Just sign here, so we can get going.

ISABELLE *(direct address/thought).* I'm going to die. My baby is going to die.

She signs the form.

Henry, I'm scared.

HENRY. I know. But it's going to be fine.

ISABELLE *(direct address/thought).* Suddenly the room is full of people. They roll my bed out into the operating suite and tip me out onto the table there. Henry is now in blue overalls and a face mask. But I can still see his eyes, he looks scared.

HENRY. Sorry, can I... hold her hand? Is that okay with the syringe?

ISABELLE (*direct address/thought*). I have to curve my spine towards the needle, arghhh... I've never been so scared in my life. But I also feel that I'm prepared to die. If they only save my baby. It's the first time I feel like a mother.

HENRY. Look at me, Isabelle, just look at me, we'll get through this.

ISABELLE (*direct address/thought*). They spray cold stuff on my belly and I have to tell them if I can still feel it, or if it's numb. If I say I can't feel it then they'll just shove a knife in. His eyes are so full of love above that green mask. I'm not looking anywhere else. My body is yanked around and something is being pushed up and down, but it's not painful, just pressure, a bit like when I had my wisdom teeth out.

HARRIET *lifts up the baby*.

HARRIET. Congratulations, it's a girl. We'll just clean her up a bit and check everything's okay, then you can hold her.

ISABELLE. Oh my God, that was quick!

HARRIET. Four minutes. They'll just sew you up now, so it'll take another twenty or so.

HENRY. Are you all right?

ISABELLE. Yeah. Yeah I think so. Bit... dazed.

HENRY. So much for our drug-free home birth, eh?

ISABELLE. Yes.

HARRIET *hands* LILY *to* HENRY, *who stands up to receive her*.

HENRY. Oh, look at her! She's perfect. See, I was right?

ISABELLE. Yes, you were. Our little Lily?

HENRY. It is indeed. Look, she's got your mouth! In miniature.

ISABELLE. Let me hold her.

HENRY *hands* LILY *to* ISABELLE.

Hello, Lily...

9.18 a.m. Tuesday 21st October 2008. ISABELLE *is cycling.*

(*Direct address/thought.*) Lily. We took her home a week later. The little hospital park with nothing but benches and concrete walkways. Pigeons... old chips trampled into the tarmac... Black metal gates. Back on the road. Oh shit. What happened there?

She stops next to SIMON, *who is hunched over on the ground, by his ghost bike, dozing.*

Hello? Did you just fall off your bike? Are you all right?

She touches him gently on the shoulder – he jerks away with a jolt.

SIMON. Hngh?

ISABELLE. Do you want me to call anyone?

SIMON. What? No, no.

ISABELLE. You're really white in the face – is it the shock? Did you hurt yourself?

SIMON. No, I just – I just woke up...

ISABELLE. Were you unconscious?

SIMON. No. Just... sleeping.

ISABELLE. Is there anything I can do?

SIMON. No, love.

ISABELLE. Anyone I can call?

SIMON. No. There's no one.

ISABELLE. You should go to A&E at least. Get yourself checked out.

SIMON. No thanks.

ISABELLE. It's just across the road...

SIMON. Trust me. They're not going to see me.

ISABELLE. I can come with you.

SIMON. You? You're the last person who can help me, you can't even help yourself.

ISABELLE. Right. Sorry… Well, I'm off then.

9.23 a.m. Tuesday 21st October 2008. ISABELLE *cycles off, determined now to go home and find* HENRY. *The encounter has thrown her off-balance.*

(*Direct address/thought.*) I'm just trying to be nice… People are just plain rude sometimes.

Shudders.

Not far now. Newsagent… Launderette… paint smeared on the kerb. I'll have a hot bath when I get home. Take Lily in with me, give her a wash. With her new duck.

Ah, here we are – I'm so happy we painted the door red – it always cheers me up. Oh, I remember when I came home from hospital with Lily, my God, the sight of this door!

21st March 2007. ISABELLE *is holding her crying baby, unsure what's wrong with her, the image of early parenthood.*

Oh, darling, shush shush shush, what's wrong, my sweet? There there, Mummy's here, it's okay. Oh oh oh, sugar pea, there there.

She smells her bottom.

No, it's not that. Do you have a hurty tummy?? There, let me rub it a bit, maybe you've got some air, hmm? Is that better? No? What can we do?

She hums a little French lullaby, 'Gardez-nous le soleil', tries to calm her down, it's not working.

Are you hungry? Is that what it is? Come here, let's see. Let's see what I've got for you.

She starts breastfeeding the baby, which calms down and drinks contentedly.

(*Great relief in her voice.*) Ahh, that's better. Of course, that's what you wanted? Silly Mama, you tried to tell me, didn't you?

9.38 a.m. Tuesday 21st October 2008. ISABELLE *arrives home.* HENRY *is in the kitchen, feeding* LILY. *He can't hear or see* ISABELLE.

HENRY. There you go, do you like that? Is that yummy?

ISABELLE (*from off*). Henry, I'm home!

HENRY. You're such a messy eater.

ISABELLE (*enters the room*). Hmm, something smells nice!

HENRY. Be patient, Lily, I've got to blow on it first, it's hot. (*Makes the sign for 'hot' – hand held in front of mouth, blows a 'H' against it.*) Yes, hot, that's right.

ISABELLE. How are you, darling?

HENRY. Porridge! Your favourite… Yes, that's right.

ISABELLE. Henry?

ISABELLE *touches* HENRY *on the shoulder. He shudders and looks behind him, but can't see her.*

HENRY. Ugh, what was that?

ISABELLE *looks at her hand, looks at* HENRY.

ISABELLE. Henry, don't do that. You're scaring me.

HENRY (*to* LILY). Have you nearly finished now?

ISABELLE (*panic-edged*). It's not funny! Stop it!

HENRY. Oh dear. You're falling asleep sitting down. Let me take you to bed.

ISABELLE. HENRY!

HENRY *carries* LILY *out of the room.*

ISABELLE *examines her body and is more and more horrified as she realises that she is no longer physically present in the world but has become a ghost. She starts breathing to control her rising panic. At the height of her distress, the bulb in the ceiling lamp explodes.* ISABELLE *turns around, stunned, and it is…*

8.30 a.m. Tuesday 21st October 2008.

A lorry comes hurtling towards her, smashes into
ISABELLE *and knocks her to the ground. The brakes*
scream as the lorry grinds to a halt. In the background,
DEBBIE *raises both hands to her mouth, exactly as before.*
Time wobbles as the light changes. ISABELLE *is pinned to*
the ground and can't move from her waist downwards, she is
momentarily unconscious. DEBBIE *comes running up to her.*
She stops short just before getting to her, takes in the scene,
swallows hard and then approaches gingerly. She is terrified,
but knows she's the first one there and must help.

DEBBIE. Oh God. Oh my... Bloody... Hello? Hello? Can you
hear me? Are you okay?

ISABELLE *mumbles something incoherent.* DEBBIE *kneels*
down next to her, takes her hand and holds it very gently. She
bends her head so it's close to ISABELLE'*s mouth.*

What did you say?

ISABELLE. Where am I?

DEBBIE. Oh, God, oh thank Christ...

ISABELLE. What happened?

DEBBIE. You were knocked off your bike. But you'll be fine.

ISABELLE. Don't leave me.

DEBBIE. No. I'll stay right here, don't you worry. How are you
feeling?

ISABELLE. I can't feel my legs.

DEBBIE. Okay. Okay... That's probably fine. Don't worry. Just
relax. Keep talking to me, that's good.

ISABELLE *tries to move, but she is trapped.*

No, don't move, don't move, just hold still, we'll have
someone here very soon.

DEBBIE *looks around to make sure someone is calling an*
ambulance, then turns her full attention back to ISABELLE.

What's your name, darling? I'm Debbie.

ISABELLE. Isabelle.

DEBBIE. Oh, that's a beautiful name!

ISABELLE. Thanks.

DEBBIE. Much nicer than Debbie. How old are you, Isabelle?

ISABELLE. Twenty-nine.

DEBBIE. Twenty-nine? That's good. You're doing so well. No, hold still. There's an ambulance on its way now. Are you uncomfortable? Hold on.

DEBBIE *takes her jumper off, folds it and places it gently under* ISABELLE'*s head.*

There, that's better, isn't it?

ISABELLE (*direct address/thought*). No. It's really not. I can barely breathe, there's something heavy pressing down on me, and something is wrong, but I can't look. You know, when one of your nails catches on something and rips off and it tears too far to where the flesh is underneath and it starts bleeding and it's just so disgusting you can't... or... cutting onions, the knife slips and goes clean through the soft pad at the top of your finger, and you can see the flap of skin and there's blood pulsing out... you just can't look at it, or you faint straight away.

DEBBIE. Isabelle!

ISABELLE (*direct address/thought*). It feels like that only a hundred times worse. I know it's bad. But I can't look.

DEBBIE. Stay with me, Isabelle, open your eyes. Darling?

ISABELLE. Yes?

DEBBIE. Come on, look at me... That's right. Good girl.

ISABELLE. I need to go now. I need to... I can't move.

DEBBIE. Oh, sweetheart, I know. I'm sorry. You just have to wait. It will be fine, we just have to... Is it work you're worried about? I can call someone, we'll sort all that out.

ISABELLE. No. (*Direct address/thought.*) Lily... I need to get home. I need to make sure she's okay.

DEBBIE. What is it then? Nothing's more important than you right now, okay? We'll need to sort you out first.

ISABELLE *starts moaning. She is clearly in a lot of pain now the shock has worn off.*

ISABELLE (*direct address/thought*). And now the pain starts rolling in. Like waves. Like being in the ocean with these huge waves crashing over me.

ISABELLE *moans loudly.*

DEBBIE (*nearly crying with distress*). Shush, darling, shush, it's going to be okay. It's going to be fine!

ISABELLE (*direct address/thought*). There's this woman, holding my hand, squeezing it. She's looking into my eyes so hard, I think she's scared to look anywhere else. I don't know her at all.

DEBBIE. You're doing so well, Isabelle, I'm proud of you.

ISABELLE (*direct address/thought*). She smells like my mum.

DEBBIE. But you must keep your eyes open, yes? Keep talking. So… do you like cycling?

ISABELLE. What?

DEBBIE. Oh sorry, sorry, I just want you to keep talking to me, just say anything that pops into your head, doesn't matter what.

ISABELLE (*moans*). Hurts.

DEBBIE. Yes, of course, it must hurt so much, but you're so brave, and you'll be absolutely fine, because they're here now, look! Just parking up. It's going to be fine.

ISABELLE. Oh my God, oh my God, I want my mum! Get her here, I want my mum!

DEBBIE. Oh, darling, I'm sorry, I'm so sorry, don't cry! Your mum will be here really soon, I promise!

ISABELLE (*direct address/thought*). I'm going under, I'm being pulled under now, I can't help it, the pull is too strong. I want to stay, I want to fight it, but everything is peaceful under the water and my limbs all go numb so I can't move and I don't want to move either, because it's so beautiful suddenly, bottle-green and then darker, blue, and darker still, and I just sink and float and it's lovely.

Pause. A shift – something has changed.

Oh.

Everything has changed.

Suddenly there's light and air and I'm back in the street, in London –

Pause as this sinks in. She gets up during the following.

– and it's all gone, the weight is gone, and there, leaning against the kerb, waiting for me, is my bike. Looking all shiny and white. I feel absolutely fine now.

ISABELLE *walks across to her bike and picks it up. She stretches, enjoying the use of her body, then starts cycling.*

The road is completely empty. All the cars are standing in a long line behind the lorry blocking the road. The police are taping off the area, and the cars are redirected. So I can just slip under the tape and have the whole road to myself. That's a novelty.

8.46 a.m. Tuesday 21st October 2008. ISABELLE cycles. She gets faster and faster, there's wind in her face. She starts humming then breaks into full-blown song, 'Don't Stop Me Now', but remembers only snatches of the lyrics.

9.50 a.m. Tuesday 21st October 2008. DEBBIE is at the police station, sitting on a chair at a desk opposite POLICE OFFICER JONES with a box of tissues at a handy distance. She is giving her witness report. ISABELLE is hurled from her bike into the scene, lands on the floor of the police station and gets up, dusting herself down.

PC JONES. Take your time. Are you sure you don't want some water?

DEBBIE. I'm fine, thanks.

ISABELLE. I'll have some.

She drinks the water. She is very thirsty. When she puts the glass down it is full of blood. The others don't notice.

PC JONES. So tell me where you work.

ISABELLE walks around the room, examining her surroundings – she has no idea why she's here.

DEBBIE. In the Oxfam shop, Kingsland Road. I heard a massive noise from outside and ran out to see what had happened.

ISABELLE looks over JONES's shoulder, who is taking notes of everything that's said. She picks up a pen, examines it. The pen breaks in two pieces. She puts it back quickly. Again, nobody notices the broken pen.

PC JONES. Do you remember the exact time?

DEBBIE. Between eight and nine, I can't remember, sorry.

PC JONES. That's fine. Go on.

DEBBIE. This woman, Isabelle…

ISABELLE. Yes?

DEBBIE. …was trapped under the wheel of the lorry. It was absurd – it looked like something from a horror film. She was conscious, well, she was slipping in and out of consciousness, but she was talking to me, and I held her hand and gave her reassurance, but I mean, everyone could see that she was…

ISABELLE stares at her.

PC JONES. I'm sorry, I know this is hard. Here.

ISABELLE. Debbie. Debbie! That's right.

He hands her the box with the tissues. DEBBIE takes one, ISABELLE does too.

DEBBIE. Thank you.

Beat. DEBBIE wipes her eyes, blows her nose. ISABELLE just looks at her tissue.

I don't think she realised though, which is a comfort, in a way. But her pelvis must have been crushed, that's where the wheel was pressing down on her, and her tummy was open, and I could see her... well, her guts, they sort of spilled out.

ISABELLE *takes her tissue and presses it to her stomach, underneath her T-shirt. When she pulls it out it is soaked in blood.*

ISABELLE. Fuck!

PC JONES. Go on.

DEBBIE. She was so young! That's what I found hardest. So young... She was very calm, really, considering what had just happened. She tried to move, but I told her it was important to keep still.

ISABELLE. Yes. I did! That's right.

PC JONES. That was good. That was the right thing.

DEBBIE. Then the fire engine came and they lifted the truck off her. A&E took her blood pressure – it was very low, barely there, and they cut off her clothes and gave her some morphine. They wanted to airlift her to hospital, but then... I think she died right there, in the road.

PC JONES. Yes, she did.

ISABELLE. Excuse me? Hello? I'm right here!

DEBBIE. In a way I'm glad it was quick, at least. For her. I mean, she didn't suffer long.

ISABELLE. Hang on, what the fuck? What are you even talking about?

DEBBIE. But what a waste.

ISABELLE. What a *waste*? This is it? This is all I get?

ISABELLE *is hurled into an adjacent interview room, which is identical to the first.*

PC MAXWELL. Take your time. Are you sure you don't want some water?

PAUL. I'm fine, thanks.

ISABELLE. Are you? Really? No, go on, have some.

ISABELLE tips the full glass over PAUL's head. He is soaked in blood, but doesn't even flinch.

PC MAXWELL. So tell me what happened.

PAUL. I checked my mirrors –

ISABELLE. Did you? Really?

PAUL. – and turned left into Forest Road and I just – felt a bump.

PC MAXWELL. Do you remember the time that happened?

ISABELLE. Who cares about the fucking time?

PAUL. Eight-thirty I think, around eight-thirty.

PC MAXWELL. And you didn't hear a scream and *then* felt the bump?

PAUL. No, not really. The radio was on. I did hear a sound from outside, but it didn't sound like a scream.

ISABELLE. Let me remind you.

She screams very loudly right in his face, he doesn't hear her.

PC MAXWELL. Okay. And what did you do then?

PAUL. I braked. I thought I'd run over a cat –

ISABELLE. Oh Jesus.

PAUL. – or that someone had put a sack of clothes into the road, or a bin bag or something.

ISABELLE. A bin bag? That's a nice touch.

PAUL. I never… I never in a million years… you know? I got out of the cab and walked around the… front of the lorry to check. First thing I saw was this woman kneeling on the ground, and I still thought it was a cat at this point, but then I saw the bike, and… and… I just think, Oh shit, oh no, oh please no no, but yes, it was. My worst nightmare.

ISABELLE. *Your* worst nightmare?

PAUL. Anyone who drives a lorry same as what I do, worst nightmare, you know?

PC MAXWELL. Go on.

ISABELLE. Why didn't you fucking look?

She grabs the broken pencil and points the jagged end at him.

PAUL. Because they're everywhere nowadays, aren't they? The roads aren't built for both, are they?

ISABELLE. Oh shut up.

She advances threateningly with the pencil in her hand.

PAUL. You stop at traffic lights, you're surrounded by them.

ISABELLE. Stop whining!

PAUL. I am so aware of it, that threat, always. Always check my mirrors, I do. But her – I just never saw her.

ISABELLE. I'm going to get you for this. Stupid stupid stupid –

She throws herself onto him with the pencil as a weapon.

PAUL. It's like she came out of nowhere.

10.04 a.m. Tuesday 21st October 2008. ISABELLE is back on her bike, cycling furiously. The sounds are a jumble of everything, traffic, birds, voices, leaves rustling, but sped-up and threatening, a wall of sound. ISABELLE needs to be back home, everything in her pulls her back.

ISABELLE *(direct address/thought)*. Please. Please, God, let this be a dream. Can't you see: I'm too young. I have a baby – you know I have a baby, you gave me that baby. Why would you do that? Give me so much happiness and then smash it just like that – I mean, it doesn't make any sense, does it? Think of my parents. I'm their child, they'll have to bury me. Henry's a widower, at thirty-three? What the fuck?

Think of Lily, she won't even remember me! She won't have any memories of her mum, growing up.

Why would you be so cruel? Why me? Why take me when there's so many others, people who've done awful things, murderers, rapists, torturers. Take one of them. Or you're just powerless and – is this about not going to church?

Or – you're not there at all. I'm just raving at nothing.

No, sorry. I didn't mean that. Of course you're there. Please be there.

What about if I started, you know, talking to you now? Praying, that sort of thing. I mean, I could go to church Sundays, couldn't I? I would – I really would! I'd do cake sales and charity things. Raise money for victims of catastrophes. Give speeches. Whatever you want me to do.

I just want to live.

Make it a dream. I promise I won't forget when I wake up.

ISABELLE *is flung back into the room where* LILY *sleeps. She quickly gets up, out of breath, and looks around.*

Oh.

She calms down and then gingerly approaches LILY*'s cot, looks into it for a while. Stretches out her hand to touch her. The child is asleep and doesn't wake from her touch.*

Lily.

My baby.

My lovely baby.

There you are.

I love you so so much.

Don't forget that.

Ever.

LILY *opens her eyes and looks at her.*

Oh. Hello?!

Can you see me?

It's me.

Mama.

You woke up… Come I'll sing your song.

ISABELLE *sings the French part of Fredrik Vahle's song 'Der Friedensmaler'.*

She can't go on.

I'll always be with you, I won't stop being your mum.

Nobody can stop me.

Nothing.

So you be a brave girl and look after your dad, okay?

Keep him busy.

He'll need you.

And I'll still look after you, I promise.

LILY *gurgles.*

You are so clever. You're the best thing that's ever happened to me. I know you'll be fine.

ISABELLE *takes off her chiffon scarf, and drops it gently into the cot.*

Take this. Keep you warm.

I love you.

Bye, sweetie, I'll just pop next door and see what Dad is up to, okay?

10.25 a.m. Tuesday 25th March 2008. ISABELLE *enters the living room.* HENRY *is sitting on the sofa, with a cup of tea and a plaster on his finger (from sweeping up the shards of glass from the exploded bulb), reading the paper. She sits down next to him.*

Did you cut yourself?

Silence.

Your finger.

Silence.

Henry. I am so sorry…

The doorbell rings. He opens the door to PC ROBERTS *and* PC MAXWELL. ISABELLE *does not leave his side.*

HENRY. Oh. Hello?

ISABELLE. Oh God. This is awful. I'm right here, okay?

PC MAXWELL. Hello. Are you… Henry Young?

HENRY. Yes?

PC MAXWELL. Could we come in, please?

HENRY. Well, it's not a good time, I've just put the baby to sleep…

ISABELLE. It's okay, Henry, let's get this over with.

PC ROBERTS (*smiles*). I understand. But it would be best if we could talk inside.

HENRY. Yes, of course, this way…

PC ROBERTS. Is anyone else in the house? Do you have any other children?

HENRY. No, no, just Lily, why?

PC MAXWELL. This the living room?

HENRY. Um. Yes. Can you tell me why you're here?

ISABELLE. Oh, God, here it comes.

PC MAXWELL. Could you just confirm, please, that Isabelle Young is your wife?

HENRY. Yes. (*Sharp in-breath.*) Oh my God.

    ISABELLE *holds* HENRY*'s hand and squeezes it hard.*

PC MAXWELL. Have you had any communication from her today?

HENRY. No. Why? Did something happen to her?

PC MAXWELL. She is dead. She was in a collision, with a lorry. I am so sorry.

HENRY. WHAT? No. No.

    ISABELLE *throws herself into* HENRY*'s arms and bursts into tears. Together they collapse onto the sofa, where* HENRY *sits, stunned, with* ISABELLE, *her legs over his and her arms still around his neck.*

PC ROBERTS. Yes. I know this is really hard to take in.

HENRY. Can I see her? I want to see her.

PC MAXWELL. Her body is at Hackney Mortuary at St John's Church.

ISABELLE. That's right next to the playground!

PC MAXWELL writes down a phone number on a pad she takes out of her bag, rips it off and puts it on the table.

PC MAXWELL. This is the number. You will have to call to find out opening times and to arrange the viewing. We can do that for you if you prefer.

She takes some leaflets out of her bag and puts them on the table.

There's some useful practical information on grief counselling in there. Have a look at them later.

PC ROBERTS. You said you have a baby? Lily?

HENRY. Yes.

ISABELLE. Yes. We do.

PC ROBERTS. How old is she?

HENRY. Eleven months.

ISABELLE. Eleven months and sixteen days. It's her birthday in two weeks.

PC ROBERTS. That's quite young, but it would still be good if you tell her what has happened. She will miss her mum and be confused and even if she doesn't fully understand, it's important for you as much as for her that you can clearly tell her. I can help you prepare that, if you like. If you want to practise...

ISABELLE. I have told her. She knows.

PC ROBERTS. You should not be alone tonight. Is there anyone you can call to be with you?

HENRY. I don't want to see anyone.

PC ROBERTS. Your parents, maybe? It's really important. We'll stay as long as you need us to. We won't leave. But think about it.

HENRY. Yes, maybe my mum. I'll call her. I just need. A couple of minutes…

PC MAXWELL. There's no rush. Take as long as you need.

Then LILY *starts crying in the other room.*

ISABELLE (*instinctively getting up to pick up her baby*). I'll go.

HENRY. I'll just get her, shall I? Bring her over here? Is that okay?

ISABELLE can't believe that she forgot that that's no longer her job.

PC ROBERTS. Absolutely.

1.45 p.m. Tuesday 21st October 2008. ISABELLE *is cycling. During the following, she revisits* SARAH, SALLY *and* SIMON *in her mind.*

SARAH. You're new here?

SALLY. Money? What's that gonna do?

SIMON. Trust me. They're not going to see me.

Now she realises that next to each of them there was a white bike decorated with flowers and cards, a ghost bike. Things click into place.

1.58 p.m. Tuesday 21st October 2008. She arrives next to SIMON. *Sits down.*

I thought you'd be back.

ISABELLE. Why didn't you tell me?

SIMON. Did you really not know?

ISABELLE. No!

SIMON. I'm sorry. You'd just woken me up. I wasn't really with it.

ISABELLE. So this is really… it?

SIMON. Um… yeah?

ISABELLE. I can't believe this. So you… and that woman, and the girl… shit.

SIMON. It took me ages too.

ISABELLE. What happened to you?

SIMON. Well, I was just cycling on, until I got to the office and everyone ignored me. Completely blanked me. I thought it was a joke.

ISABELLE. Oh shit.

SIMON. Exactly.

ISABELLE. And how did you...?

SIMON. Lorry.

ISABELLE. Me too.

SIMON. When?

ISABELLE. This morning.

SIMON. Oh, fuck. Today? I'm sorry.

ISABELLE. It's okay. Thank you. And you?

SIMON. Nearly five years now? I think. June.

ISABELLE. And... how is it?

SIMON. Well, I'm mostly just here now. There's no point in going anywhere, is there?

ISABELLE. So this is it? We just sit here?

SIMON. Well, you don't have to.

ISABELLE. But that's crazy.

SIMON. Yeah, well. What can you do? Nice of you to stop by. Bit of a change. Where are you?

ISABELLE. What do you mean?

SIMON. Where will they put your bike?

ISABELLE. My bike?

SIMON. Where did it happen? Where were you killed?

ISABELLE. Oh. Kingsland Road. By the Oxfam.

SIMON. Okay. Maybe I'll drop by some time.

ISABELLE. That would be nice.

They sit in silence.

I don't really know what to do now.

SIMON. Just stay. As long as you want.

ISABELLE. I normally feel things – like I feel tired, or hungry, or cold and then I know what to do... But it's been all day and that's all gone.

I'm still sad though.

Angry.

SIMON. That'll go too.

ISABELLE. Is that a good thing?

SIMON. No point being angry – nothing we can do about it now...

ISABELLE. There must be something we can do. There's so many of us, all over London.

SIMON. So what, you're going to start a revolution?

ISABELLE. Why not?

4.30 p.m. 15th November 2008, dark outside. The white bike is tied to a lamp post. HENRY arrives with some flowers and a bag. He looks at the bike for a while. Shakes his head. It's about a week after all the family and friends have put the bike up, and about ten days after the funeral. This is the first time he is alone with her. ISABELLE is reading the cards left by her bike.

HENRY. Hey. You.

ISABELLE. Henry!

She puts her cards down, and gets up.

HENRY. I've come back. Brought you these.

ISABELLE. Oh. Thank you!

HENRY. I never really bought you flowers, did I? Always thought it was naff. Ah well, here you are.

ISABELLE. They're beautiful!

Gives him a hug. He shivers.

HENRY. At last. Bit too late.

HENRY *puts the flowers down, then buries his head in his hands, pulls at his hair, makes a strangled sound.*

This is crazy. What am I doing?

ISABELLE (*tenderly*). Oh, Henry. It's good to talk! You *should* talk to me... it's very healthy.

HENRY. You can't be dead. I just don't believe it.

ISABELLE. I know. Weird, eh?

HENRY. So, where are you?

ISABELLE. I'm just... here. Keeping busy.

HENRY. We need you.

ISABELLE. I know.

HENRY. Every morning, before I wake up properly, I could swear you're lying next to me. I can feel your warmth.

ISABELLE. Yes. I am, actually.

HENRY. And then I open my eyes and remember.

ISABELLE. Henry... I'm not going anywhere. I'm still around. You know that. Why would you talk to me otherwise?

HENRY. I haven't even moved your jeans from the bedroom floor. They're crumpled up on your side of the bed. They look as if they're waiting for you. Your book is half-read, face-down. Your pillow still smells of you. It's so hard, just getting up in the morning.

ISABELLE. And with nobody to bring you your coffee, eh?

HENRY. You walked out the door that morning, and then – bang. I'm still waiting for you to come back.

ISABELLE. Well, I'm doing my best. If there's any way, I will.

HENRY. Sometimes I think, if I just walk out into the traffic.

ISABELLE. What?

HENRY. Everything I look at turns into a portal, to where you are. Razors.

ISABELLE. Hang on, Henry, don't even think shit like that!

HENRY. Tube train.

ISABELLE. Are you crazy? What about Lily?

HENRY. Kitchen knife.

ISABELLE. Listen to me, Henry. Stop this. Now!

HENRY. Bathroom cabinet full of pills.

> ISABELLE *touches him, holds both his hands. He shivers violently, but this throws him out of his reverie.*

I won't do it, of course. Too much of a coward.

ISABELLE. Good.

HENRY. I just think Lily would be better off without me. I'm a wreck.

ISABELLE. You are her father. Okay? You are sad, you are grieving, you're going through the shittest time of your life, but so is she. She needs you. And you need her. And you will be fine. Okay? I can't believe you're doing this! I'd give anything, anything, to be alive again, and you want to just throw it all away? It's not my fault this happened. Don't make it worse for me now.

> HENRY *buries his head in his hands.*

HENRY. I'm sorry. That was an awful thing to say. I promise I'll look after her.

ISABELLE. You'd better! Or I will haunt you for real, just you wait!

HENRY. What are we going to do?

ISABELLE. Well, I'm not going to just lie down and take it, believe me.

HENRY. You're dead. The whole world should just stop. All this traffic just keeps going. The sun keeps shining. I see old couples holding hands and I just want to hit them – it's so unfair. What about us? What about you and me?

ISABELLE. Of course, it's shit, isn't it. I'd give anything just to touch you and for you to feel it.

HENRY. Since you died, I've had this pain, inside me, like an animal burrowing deep inside. I ache because I'm empty. It's like someone took a big spoon and just scraped out my core. I just ache. All the time.

ISABELLE. And soon I won't be able to feel anything.

HENRY. I brought you something else.

He pulls out ISABELLE's *chiffon scarf, smells it. As he does so, she steps so close to him that he can smell her. They don't touch, both have their eyes closed and keep very still, savouring the moment. They both open their eyes – as if they're about to kiss. But then, with an abrupt movement, he takes the scarf and ties it around the handlebar of the white bike.* ISABELLE *steps back at this.*

ISABELLE. I love you, Henry, and you love me. And we both love Lily. So this is not the end. We'll just keep going.

6.15 p.m. 29th November 2013. HENRY *is outside the TfL Headquarters. He is pushing his bike along. There's a crowd of people. He stops, tries to see what's happening at the front. The noise of helicopters overhead, whistles and many people talking.* LILY, *six years old, walks beside him, pushing her bike. Someone is reading a list of names, muffled.*

HENRY. Wow, that's a lot of people, eh?

I think they're reading the names out now.

LILY. I can't hear anything!

HENRY. Let's go to the front.

The list of names becomes clearer. It includes ISABELLE's *name. As the name is read out, she steps on stage, with her white bike. The list continues for two or three names, in alphabetic order.* ISABELLE *moves slowly towards* HENRY *and* LILY. *She looks at them. Suddenly a hush falls over the crowd and everyone starts ringing their bike bells.*

Ah, it's starting now. (*Hands her a hot-water bottle from a rucksack.*) Put it under your jumper. It's freezing.

LILY *does so.*

Just lie down with me and try not to move, okay? We'll have to be really quiet, and not say anything.

LILY. Okay.

HENRY. If you get too cold, just climb on top of me, I can be your mattress.

Then they all lay down their bikes and lie down next to them on the ground, pretending they're dead. HENRY *and* LILY *lie down too.* ISABELLE *puts her bike on top of theirs and lies down between them.*

LILY. What's that tower?

HENRY. It's a big office. The people who work there can make things safer on the roads.

So that people don't get killed any more.

LILY. Like Mum?

HENRY. Yes. Like Mum. Shhh, we have to be quiet now. Close your eyes.

LILY *and* HENRY *close their eyes. They lie very still.*

ISABELLE. That's my old coat! I haven't seen that on you before. Mum must have kept it for all these years...

You look so lovely, Lily.

She kisses her, LILY *smiles.*

My little chick.

She turns to HENRY.

And how are you today, my love? I think you're doing a great job, you know. I am seriously proud of you. Of us. Our little family.

She strokes his face, kisses his hand. Then looks around her.

It's amazing... Look! Everyone's here. They all came!

All these people. And all of us too. The white bikes scattered over the real ones, like fog rising from the ground. There's so many people here! All these faces quiet and calm.

Is that guy crying? There's a tear rolling down now, bless him. He doesn't even have a ghost with him.

Oh, look up there! They're all looking down at us. TfL Headquarters looks like a glass tower from a fairytale. And all these people have left their desks and are standing by the full-length windows, like cut-out dolls, looking down at us, lying in the road.

And the people coming out of the Tube all stand round the edge and take pictures and look. It's quiet. This is a busy junction normally. Amazing to see it empty of cars, and full of people. Lying down.

It feels good, this. We're all together, all of us.

The dead and the living.

Because we want the same thing.

To be safe.

We're all still here.

And today for the first time since it happened, I think we all feel seen.

These silhouettes of men and women behind glass, holding cappuccinos and files, they look down at us lying here, and I think they can see us. I can feel their eyes on me.

Feels warm, like sunshine on skin.

I count.

We all count.

And that is an amazing feeling.

The End.

THE VILLAGE CHURCH

Characters

TOM, *late sixties, old commie*
MARIE, *mid-fifties, bubbly and sociable*
ZOE, *their daughter, early thirties and a breath of fresh air*

It's dark.

We hear the last stanza of the hymn 'As We Gather at Your Table', sung by many voices at a village church service. It's ephemeral, beautiful, a bit haunting.

Lights up on TOM, *in corduroys, a nice shirt, glasses on a chain round his neck and a flowery pink-and-blue Cath Kidston apron that has seen better days. The hymn fades into Radio 4, from a transistor radio on the kitchen counter. He stirs a big Le Creuset pot on the Aga, then looks into an old and stained cookery book on the counter, finds he can't see properly, fumbles for his glasses, and awkwardly puts them on.*

He reads.

TOM. Ah. Shit.

He reads a bit more.

Where the fuck do I get bay leaves from?

He chuckles.

A bouquet garni? I am so sorry to disappoint… how remiss of me.

He leaves the kitchen through the front door, which opens directly onto a stone-flagged path surrounded by green. We can hear birds, and sunlight falls in through the open door. A few seconds later he returns triumphantly with some sprigs of rosemary and thyme in his fist. He leaves the door ajar.

Aha!

He crumbles the herbs between thumb and finger, smells them and has a moment over it.

That'll do.

He uses a mortar and pestle to soften the herbs and release their aroma. He hums a little ditty. He puts the herbs into the pot, stirs, and tastes a bit off the wooden spoon. It's perfect.

The door opens, and ZOE *is in. She is life itself, and launches herself at her dad.*

ZOE. Dad!

TOM. Squirt!

They embrace.

ZOE. You okay?

TOM. Never been better. Good to see you.

ZOE. And you! Nice apron. Suits you.

He takes it off and hangs it on a hook. ZOE *starts laying the table.* MARIE *enters with some daffodils she's picked in the garden, puts them in a glass milk bottle, adds water from the tap and puts them on the table.*

TOM. Food's almost done. I'll just get the wine up.

He leaves through the other door.

ZOE. He looks fine to me.

MARIE. Because you're here. He's a grumpy old sod most of the time.

ZOE. This smells gorgeous.

MARIE. Yeah, he got better at cooking, I'll give him that.

ZOE. Well, just talk to him.

MARIE. I have! He doesn't listen.

ZOE. Just tell him how you feel.

MARIE. He doesn't care. You'll see. He's just getting more and more stubborn.

ZOE. Oh, Mum, stop it. He's fine.

MARIE. Maybe if you bring it up... we're in a rut about it.

ZOE. Okay, I can mention it. But I'm not doing your dirty work for you.

TOM *clatters up the stairs and through the door with two dusty wine bottles. Throughout the following they sit down and start serving themselves.* TOM *uncorks a bottle and pours three generous glasses.*

Wow, you're ambitious.

MARIE. Oh, we'll get through it.

TOM. Saves me going down halfway through the meal.

ZOE. Smells amazing, is that chicken?

TOM. Coq au vin.

MARIE. Pass me the baguette, please.

ZOE. Have you been outside yet, Dad? It's gorgeous. Summery.

TOM. Yes. I have, actually. The herbs are from our garden.

ZOE. That was it? An excursion three steps out of your front door?

TOM. Well, I've been working hard, slaving over the stove.

MARIE. He was still asleep when I left.

TOM. Because I work at night. I was up until two. Your mother doesn't appreciate me enough.

ZOE. Oh, pooh.

TOM. She doesn't.

ZOE. I thought you were retired, Dad? What are you working on?

MARIE. He's 'writing a book'.

TOM. What? I am.

MARIE. I know you are.

TOM. Then don't put it in inverted commas.

MARIE. I did no such thing.

ZOE. But that's great, Dad! What kind? Novel?

TOM. No, not exactly.

ZOE. What then?

TOM. Oh, it's complicated. Defies categorisation. I'll put a label on it when I have to.

MARIE. Nobody makes you work until two in the morning. You have all day, every day.

TOM. Oh, but the muse is elusive, isn't she.

MARIE. He's just watching porn.

ZOE. Mum!

TOM (*indignantly*). I am not! I was on a roll. I wrote two thousand words.

MARIE. But were they any good?

TOM. The problem with your mother is – she has no faith in me.

MARIE. I just wish you would engage a bit more in village life, that's all. You're becoming a recluse. Hannah and Adam didn't even seem to know I was married. They sort of vaguely treated me as a widow. Sort of on spec. Wanted me to come to the bingo.

ZOE. Oh yes. Mum seems to know half the village.

MARIE. Because I go to church!

TOM. Oh please.

ZOE. Well, it wouldn't hurt you to show your face a bit more, Dad. Why don't you go along some time?

TOM. Marie, did you put her up to this?

MARIE. Me, no.

TOM. Zoe, sweetie, you know how I abhor all that… mumbo-jumbo. Don't you start as well.

ZOE. Yes, I know, Dad, but it's not about that here, is it?

TOM. Well, what is it about then?

ZOE. It's just about village life – that's where people socialise. And if you remove yourself from it, then you don't get involved, you'll never get to know people.

MARIE. Darling, it would be nice if you came along, and supported me with what I am trying to do here. Make some friends. As a couple. We need to show we're willing to engage, that's what you get when you move to a village, it revolves

around the church. Quizzes, fundraisers, coffee mornings.
They think we're snobbish Londoners if we don't go.

TOM. We are!

MARIE. We're not! We're here now. For good.

TOM. Look, I didn't say anything when the two of you
gallivanted off this morning –

MARIE. Because you were asleep –

TOM. Or when you came back, glowing with holier-than-thou
Christianity –

MARIE. Oh come off it!

TOM. But if you really want my opinion, I think it is
hypocritical and downright wrong.

ZOE. Why?

TOM. Do you believe?

ZOE. Well…

MARIE. I do actually.

TOM. Really?

MARIE. Yes.

TOM. In a virgin conceiving and her child walking on water,
healing the dead, then being murdered but undead pushing
away the tombstone and rising up to heaven?

MARIE. What it says in the Bible and Christian belief are two
different things.

ZOE. Dad, you are deliberately trying to be difficult.

TOM. I can tell you what my problem is. It's not the Bible, it's
the fact that faith is blind. The Bible is just pushing it that
one step further. Testing how little you can see.

ZOE. What?

TOM. Like an optometrist. Is it blurrier like this? Or like this?
Do you get a fuzzy warm feeling now? Or now? Are the
facts sufficiently clouded yet? The Church has been

exploiting people's inherent need for faith and guidance for
centuries, and abused it in the pursuit of power.

MARIE. Look, Tom, the basic values of the Church of England
are good. Love thy neighbour, do good in the world… give
to the poor. I believe in that.

TOM. It's sanctimonious bullshit –

ZOE. Being friendly with the people around you and looking
after the poor is bullshit?

TOM. Feeling superior because you are following a rule book
that tells you to behave in a certain way is. Looking down on
everyone who doesn't live by your rules is. Excluding people
from your social circle because they don't go to church is.

MARIE. Because nobody ever sees you.

TOM. I go shopping! I go for walks! Plenty of people see me.
Nobody ever talks to me.

MARIE (*to* ZOE). Look how peeved he is about it.

ZOE. That's probably because they don't know who you are.
You know there's coffee in church after? They all stand
around and natter.

MARIE. I just don't understand why you have to make this so
difficult for both of us.

TOM. I'm not!

MARIE. We moved here over a year ago now. There's a limit to
what I can do when I work all week. And still I have managed
to create some kind of network – not at all helped by you, who
has all the time in the world now, but lack motivation.

TOM. Well, I am sorry. I am just deeply suspicious of belief
systems. I don't want to be pulled into one, just because
you're a bit bored in the countryside.

ZOE. Dad, that's ridiculous. You're not being radicalised by the
village church. You drink some coffee, you hum along to
some songs, you listen to the priest, that's it.

TOM. I am glad you mention radicalisation – what's the
difference between ISIS and our village church?

MARIE. ISIS? Psshhh.

ZOE. What?

TOM. Each tells you that if you fight in their corner, you'll have eternal life. Each asks you to believe unquestioningly the rules they have invented and try to impose on the world. Take Trump!

ZOE. Oh no, can we not?

MARIE. He will always bring Trump into it eventually.

ZOE. I have even stopped listening to the news, I'm so depressed.

TOM. Alternative facts. He wants you to believe. Trust. Have faith in only him. And the only way he can do that is by discrediting everyone who tries to point out that what he says is a lie, and that they can prove it because the facts are there. For all to see.

MARIE. How can you compare –

TOM. It's all the same thing! If someone asks you to close your eyes to the truth and just believe their version of events and follow their rules, it's the same thing. It's dangerous. And I'm not doing it.

ZOE. I get your point, but come on, you're talking about the village church. I don't think there could be anything more harmless! There are ducks in the pond, it's idyllic.

TOM. Don't be fooled, my child. What's-his-name, the young chap, curly hair, you know…

ZOE. The priest?

TOM. Yes, but he's got a name, doesn't he?

MARIE. Everyone just calls him the priest.

TOM. Yes, see, he's become something institutional – a function, he's not even an individual any more. Because if he was just plain Mr Smith –

MARIE. He's not called Smith.

TOM. I'm just making a point here. If people call him Mr Smith or whatever, he would be someone with mere opinions,

someone flawed, fallible, human. But like this, he's THE
PRIEST who is leading his CONGREGATION, he is
somehow more than... he has the weight of the Church behind
him. Such a shrimp, but he carries the weight of thousands of
years of crusades and plundering and cutting people's tongues
out and buggering choirboys and amassing gold and building
cathedrals and that is what gives him... gives him...

ZOE. Dad?

TOM.... authority.

ZOE. You okay, Dad?

TOM. I'm... fine.

*He clearly isn't. His face has changed colour and his
breathing has become laborious. His knuckles on the table
cloth are turning white.*

MARIE. See what I have to put up with?

ZOE. I don't think...

*TOM very slowly slides off his seat. One side of his mouth is
pulled downwards.*

MARIE. Tom?

ZOE. Shit, Mum, is he having –

*MARIE jumps up and catches TOM before he hits the floor.
Everything becomes sped up and very slow at the same time.
She is crouching with his upper body and head in her arms,
his lower body is awkwardly folded under the table.*

MARIE. Quick, dial nine-nine-nine. Where's your mobile?

*ZOE runs over to where her coat and bag are and rummages
around in her bag. The phone is not there. Eventually she
finds it in her coat pocket.*

Tom, can you hear me? I'm here, I've got you. You'll be
okay. You silly bugger, you.

ZOE. Fuck fuck fuck, where is it?

MARIE. If you can't find it, mine is upstairs, charging.

ZOE. It must be here, come on, fuck.

MARIE. Stop swearing, Zoe, stop it. Let's be calm.

ZOE. Oh fucking crap!

MARIE. I've got you, darling. We'll sort you out.

ZOE. Here!

She dials with flying fingers.

TOM. Mmmmh. Mmmmmh.

MARIE. What's that? Darling?

TOM. Mh mmmmh mmh.

MARIE. I know. I know. I love you too.

ZOE. Hello? Yes, I think my father is having a heart attack.

TOM. Kkkk. Pppp.

MARIE. Try not to speak. Save your energy. Don't agitate yourself.

ZOE. Apple Tree Cottage. The Street. Hang on...

ZOE leaves the room, and closes the door. MARIE starts crying as she strokes TOM's hair and face.

MARIE. You silly old fool. Don't you dare. Don't you dare leave me.

TOM. Mmmmarie.

MARIE. Yes! Tom, yes, that's good, I'm here.

TOM. I nnnnnnd...

MARIE. Yes?

TOM. I nnnnnneed...

He is exhausted, and has a rest, closes his eyes.

MARIE. I know, you need an ambulance, it's on its way, Zoe is sorting it right now, just relax. Save your strength.

TOM. Mmmh. A... mmmh a –

ZOE comes back into the room, rushes over to MARIE and TOM.

ZOE. How is he?

MARIE. Shhh. He's trying to say something.

ZOE. Dad?

> ZOE *holds his hand, he squeezes it. Then lies back completely still.*

I love you, Dad.

MARIE. He knows that. He loves you too.

ZOE. Oh my God. Is he…

MARIE. Shhhh.

He'll pull through. He's strong.

TOM. Mmmh… Nnnneeed… Pppppp.

ZOE. Oh this is awful.

> ZOE *moves so that she is looking straight into his face,* MARIE *and* ZOE *are facing each other, with* TOM *in the middle. The plates and glasses are on the table above them.*

TOM. Ppppprrrr.

MARIE. Yes, darling? What do you want? What do you need?

> TOM *pulls himself up onto his elbows, raises his head and looks at* ZOE *with real urgency in his eyes.*

TOM. Ppppriest.

> MARIE *and* ZOE *look at each other with complete disbelief.*

> *Blackout.*

> *In the darkness, we hear the opening stanza of the hymn 'Abide With Me', sung by many voices at a service in a village church.*

> *The End.*

BABY DOLLS

Baby Dolls was first performed at Hackney Attic, London, as part of the East End Literary Salon, in June 2015, with the following cast:

MOLLY	Shakella Dedi
NATASHA	Jemma Moore
JOANNE	Grace Edwards
Director	Milla Jackson

Characters

MOLLY
JOANNE
NATASHA

We are at a baby shower, at MOLLY*'s place. There are
sandwiches on the table, a few baby-gros unwrapped, a nappy
cake, lots of pink, and wrapping paper. Half-empty glasses.*
MOLLY *is six months pregnant, and in the kitchen.*

On the sofa are JOANNE *and* NATASHA. JOANNE *is absent-
mindedly rocking a small pram from which a baby's screaming
is heard, and* NATASHA *is busy typing a text into her phone.*
MOLLY *appears with a large platter full of cupcakes, all
decorated lavishly, with different-coloured icing and sprinkles.
She's wearing a frilly apron, and looks flushed.*

MOLLY. Ta-dah!

  *Nobody takes notice, they're both too wrapped up in what
  they are doing.*

  Ta-dah!!!

JOANNE. Oh, wow, Molly! Good work. Do you remember
  how you get her to shut up?

MOLLY. These are butter cream, and these are normal cream,
  and the pink ones are royal icing.

  NATASHA *pings off her message, it makes a zingy sound.
  She looks around.*

JOANNE. I just can't get her to stop! Rocking is good, isn't it?

NATASHA. What are you trying to do to us? Heart attack? Or
  just fat thighs?

MOLLY. Or you could pick her up.

JOANNE. What, like, take her out?

MOLLY. Yes, just put her on your shoulder, pat her back a bit?

NATASHA. Or take the battery out?

  JOANNE *gets up and peers cautiously into the pram. She's
  unsure how to approach the screaming bundle.* MOLLY
  picks the doll up and puts her over her shoulder. The

screaming stops immediately. She passes the doll over to
JOANNE, *who nervously keeps her in a similar position.*

MOLLY. See, that worked.

JOANNE. Thank you.

NATASHA. Yes and thank *God* my eardrums are still intact –
just… Can you hear that ringing?

JOANNE. I just can't think properly when she screams like that.

MOLLY. You'll learn. It gets easier. How long have you had
her now?

JOANNE. Three months.

MOLLY. Gets easier after the first year. I have to say, I miss
mine, now she's gone.

NATASHA. Please tell me that's not true!

MOLLY. It's strange, I've been looking forward to this –
(*Points at her belly.*) for so long, and now it feels unreal.

NATASHA. Really? I thought it would finally feel real – at least
you know that's not plastic in there, don't you?

MOLLY. Yes, but I can't see her face.

JOANNE. I see *her* face far too much – especially at three in the
morning. Sometimes I feel that it's all a big joke, that there's
some bloke sitting somewhere in this control room, pissing
himself every time he wakes me up with the feeding scream.

Tash, tell me, I look grey, don't I? I think I've aged at least
two years in the last few months.

NATASHA. Well…

MOLLY. No you don't, of course you don't, you look lovely.
You've done so well! You have to look at the bigger picture.

JOANNE. Yes, I know. Oh God…

The doll starts whimpering.

What is it *now*?

MOLLY. Try the bottle.

MOLLY *holds the doll very gently, while* JOANNE *rifles through her pram bag in rising panic.*

JOANNE. Where is it? Come on… I know I've packed it. Come on!

MOLLY. If you can't find it, I've got an old one in the kitchen.

JOANNE. No, here it is!

NATASHA. Hooray.

MOLLY. Tash.

JOANNE (*is now 'feeding' the doll with a plastic bottle*). What is with you, Tash? You'll have to do this as well, you know?

NATASHA. Do I?

JOANNE. Well, if you ever want to have kids. Not that young any more…

NATASHA. I'm twenty-five, for Christ's sake!

JOANNE. Just saying, takes at least three years with the doll, and that's if you pass all the tests, and then you still need to get pregnant, not everyone's as fertile as Molly.

NATASHA. Yes, Molly, I've wanted to ask you – *how* did you get pregnant exactly? What's the trick?

MOLLY. You know I can't talk about it.

JOANNE. Yeah I know, but… does it hurt?

MOLLY. No, well maybe the first time… and the second, but then it's fine.

NATASHA. You're talking about sex, right?

JOANNE. I don't mean that! I mean what they do to you.

NATASHA. Is it an operation or something? Are you conscious?

MOLLY. What? No! No, course not.

NATASHA. Do they implant, or inject you?

MOLLY. No, it's all natural. It's like it always was.

JOANNE. What? I can't believe that.

NATASHA. It doesn't work the old-fashioned way for the rest of us, I can tell you.

MOLLY. But you wouldn't know, you're not married. (*To* JOANNE.) I think you need to change her now.

NATASHA. So?

JOANNE. You sure? (*Smells the baby doll's bottom.*)

MOLLY. Natasha. You're not…

NATASHA. So am. Purely for research of course.

JOANNE. Cool…

MOLLY. But that's like… totally illegal!

NATASHA. Look, I never made the rules.

MOLLY. But it's so dangerous.

JOANNE. Yeah you could get an STD, or you could get stabbed or… or anything could happen!

NATASHA. I'm not saying I just sleep with strangers, am I?

MOLLY. Who then? I don't believe you, Tash. You're just having us on.

JOANNE. No, I think she's… Aren't you scared they'll find out?

NATASHA. Look, I'm going to tell you something. But you have to *swear* not to tell anyone about this, ever.

MOLLY. I don't know if I want to know actually.

JOANNE. I do. And I swear.

NATASHA. Molly?

JOANNE. Well, go into the kitchen if you don't want to know. Go, change Thingy here. (*Hands her the doll.*)

MOLLY. You haven't even named her yet?

JOANNE. I just couldn't think of anything!

MOLLY. You are unbelievable.

MOLLY *takes the doll and starts to leave the room with her. It's clear she is full of maternal feelings for the doll and pities her for being with* JOANNE.

JOANNE. Come on, Tash, what is it?

NATASHA. I kind of need to tell both of you. Or nobody.

JOANNE. Really, why?

NATASHA. Molly? Can you stay?

MOLLY. Okay then. (*Sighs.*) Go on.

JOANNE. You have to swear.

MOLLY. Okay then, I swear.

NATASHA. Well, haven't you been curious about why nobody gets pregnant any longer?

JOANNE. What? Duh. (*Points at* MOLLY'*s belly.*)

NATASHA. I mean, naturally.

MOLLY. Well, it was natural, actually.

NATASHA. Okay, maybe it was natural, in that you suddenly conceived after having sex with your husband, but only because you went down the official routes, didn't you? You were full of stamps, literally all over your body. Passed all your tests. Did the formative-year test run, had the physical, the mental assessment, showed them the marriage certificate, right?

MOLLY. Well yes, you've got to – otherwise they won't know you'll do a good job, will they?

Pointed look at JOANNE, *whom she clearly thinks is not doing a good job. She then starts unwrapping the nappy cake on the table, to prepare for the nappy change.*

NATASHA. Yeah, but what has that done to you? Will caring for a plastic doll for three years really make you into a better mother? Will that prepare you?

MOLLY. Well, they say that nothing can prepare you for having children, but surely this is as good a way as possible? In the past there were women who had ten children, no money and no idea how to look after them. At least that's not happening any longer.

NATASHA. Okay, but what's happening to instinct? To spontaneity? To making love and happening to get pregnant and it turns your life around for the better.

MOLLY. Excuse me, but that's just sentimental romantic bullshit.

NATASHA. What's it like for you now, Jo? Feeling blissfully happy?

JOANNE. You know what? You're right. (*To* MOLLY.) She's right! I feel rubbish. I don't know what to do with it. I was excited in the beginning, but then after a week of no sleep and nothing coming back, no smile, no gurgle, just this impassive... plastic mask... I started to resent it. I *hope*, I really hope it will get better soon, or I'll fling it against the wall some day!

MOLLY. No, you won't! It's normal to feel like that in the beginning. You'll start to love her soon.

JOANNE. Will I? Really? I don't know if I want to love her. She's plastic.

MOLLY (*covers the doll's ears*). Shush, don't say that, she's only small, but she can hear you!

NATASHA. Okay, let me tell you a secret, yeah? I have a partner. We're not married or anything, and we haven't applied for any tests or anything, and nobody knows we're together. But we have been trying for a baby for two years now. And nothing's happening.

MOLLY. Tash! How could you! Of course nothing's happening... babies come from God, don't they? He's not going to give you one, if you're trying to conceive in sin.

NATASHA. Well, maybe babies used to come from God or whatever, more likely not, but okay, let's call it God, Love, Nature, whatever you like. But that's not where they come from now.

JOANNE. What do you mean?

NATASHA. Well, isn't it clear as day? The Government decides who is fit to be a parent and who isn't. They feed us all this bullshit about marriage as the only way and God, and having to prove your worth – but what are they actually doing? *How* are they preventing everyone else from getting knocked up? That's what I would like to know.

Silence.

JOANNE. Well, actually, I've been wondering as well. Martin and I... well, we knew we wanted to get married at some point, but we also, you know... before. And... nothing happened. For years.

MOLLY. You had premarital sex, for years? I mean, to be honest, I'm not surprised Tash has, but you... and Martin? Why?

JOANNE. Because we wanted to have a baby together, without anyone telling us how to. Because I didn't like the idea of having to pretend to be a mum to a piece of plastic and be monitored by health-care visitors and told off at every opportunity when what I was doing had nothing to do with looking after my own baby, and was just an absurd farce! That's why.

NATASHA. Bravo. Well said.

MOLLY. I'm not going to listen to this any longer. I'm going to go and change her now, since you clearly don't care! I should call the police, the way you're talking.

MOLLY *leaves the room, clutching the baby.*

JOANNE. Do you think she will?

NATASHA. She won't.

JOANNE. They could have me for neglect as well.

NATASHA. She just had to make a point.

MOLLY (*from outside*). I can still hear you, you know? And don't be so sure I won't do it. If I don't say anything I'll be just as guilty as the two of you, and in my situation...

JOANNE *and* NATASHA *look at one another. They instinctively know that there is only one way forward. They both stretch out their hands to take a cupcake.* MOLLY *comes back in with the doll as they take their first bite.*

NATASHA (*with her mouth full*). Hmm, Molly, this is… amazing.

JOANNE. Really yummy. How did you make these?

MOLLY. You want the recipe? You don't bake, do you?

JOANNE. I think I might start, now that…

NATASHA. Molly, you could sell these, you know.

MOLLY (*hands the doll back to* JOANNE). Here you go. Nice and dry.

JOANNE. Thanks, Molly. (*To the doll.*) Do you want some milky-milk now?

MOLLY. I think she needs a nap. She was dropping off on the changing mat.

JOANNE. Was she? Okay, lie down, my little love. Sleep tight. There we go.

NATASHA. You're a good teacher, Moll.

MOLLY. Okay, stop it, you two. I know it's wrong, but I won't say anything. So stop the act.

NATASHA *and* JOANNE *quickly but discreetly put down their cupcakes.* JOANNE, *who was gazing lovingly into the pram, abruptly looks elsewhere.*

NATASHA. There's something else.

MOLLY. What?

NATASHA. Do you think… I could stay with you for a bit?

MOLLY. No way. Don't even think about it.

NATASHA. You know I wouldn't ask if it wasn't really important.

JOANNE. You can stay with us…

NATASHA. Thanks, Joanne, I appreciate it, but it has to be Molly.

MOLLY. Why? Are you crazy?

JOANNE. It wouldn't be a problem.

NATASHA. You are being monitored, Jo. Your house isn't safe. (*Indicates the doll now asleep in the pram.*)

JOANNE. Oh. Yeah.

MOLLY. Do you have any idea what I'm going through right now?

Do you know what it's like to lug this around all day, to have hormones zinging round your body, to feel constantly terrified something will happen. I have to watch what I put in my mouth every minute of the day, I can't use… insect repellent… window cleaner… I'm a liability. My nerves are shot as it is. I really, and I mean *really* don't need a wanted criminal on the hit list living under my roof right now, thank you very much.

Sorry.

NATASHA. No, no, it's fine. Say it like it is.

JOANNE. Oh God, Molly, you never said… is that what it's like for you?

MOLLY. And I'm fucking terrified of the birth – it's going to be a bloodbath. And if I survive it, I'll have tears and saggy boobs and my body will never, never be the same again. And I've been so *good*, I've followed all the rules, I should just feel lucky lucky lucky every day of this amazing wonderful 'time of my life' time.

NATASHA. But you're not. See?

JOANNE. I'm so sorry, Molly!

MOLLY (*sobbing*). No I'm fucking *not*! I get tension headaches and and I'll probably have varicose veins next, and I'll actually shit myself during the birth – do you know that's what they call 'natural' and Phil will be there to record it all on video and – oh fuck it, I just feel completely and utterly TRAPPED by it all. I'm really don't know what I'm doing AT ALL!

JOANNE. Shh, shh, it's okay, Molly, I'm sure you'll be brilliant at it – come here. Shall I give you a massage? It's normal to feel down like that sometimes. Probably the hormones, what do you think?

NATASHA. No, you're right, Molly, that's exactly what's happening. Couldn't have said it better myself. We're being manipulated. We're being sold off cheaply. We're just empty vessels. We're being fed complete bullshit. And we have to do something – we have to claim back our territory.

MOLLY. But how? It's far too late now, surely?

NATASHA. No, it's perfect. You're off the monitors, I'll sleep on your sofa, we'll tell Phil it's because my mum died, and I'll be ever so good and help you with the house and everything, I promise, he'll love it… and I can go completely under the radar.

JOANNE. And what do I do?

NATASHA. Well, you're our guinea pig.

JOANNE. No way.

NATASHA. Think about it – if you can keep it up with Thingy and pass all your exams and everything, and Molly can help you with that – then you'll be next in line. And we'll be systematic. We monitor everything you eat, drink, take into your body –

MOLLY. Tash!

NATASHA. Well, okay, not everything, but you know what I mean. We need to find out how they do it. What it is that makes them choose. How they make our bodies infertile or fertile at will. We'll be a sleeper cell. We'll be our own private detectives.

JOANNE. I don't know – it sounds incredibly dangerous.

MOLLY. It sounds crazy.

NATASHA. But don't you want to know?

JOANNE. Well…

MOLLY. Absolutely no way!

NATASHA. Moll, I've been watched. They're watching my house. I can't go back.

JOANNE. Shit. That's… Really? Why would they do that?

NATASHA. I must be on to something… It is kind of a good sign, well, good and bad.

I have a theory, you know?

MOLLY. No actually, I don't want to know.

JOANNE. What? What is it? You think you know how they do it.

NATASHA. Yep. I think it's in the water. There's something in the tap water, and then, there's not. Or there's something else.

MOLLY (*holding her ears closed*). Lalalalalala.

NATASHA. I am pretty sure it's that. Maybe in the bread as well.

JOANNE. That sounds crazy!

NATASHA. Why else do they scan your card at the bakery before they serve you? Molly, did the bread taste different, or did it have a different texture after you'd passed the test? Did you notice anything being different? What about the water? Did anyone come round, a plumber or someone?

MOLLY. I'm not even going to answer that. That's ridiculous.

NATASHA. That means yes, right? Come on, Molly, you can tell us!

MOLLY *refuses, it's clear she's scared. She gestures that she will whisper it in their ears, but says:*

MOLLY. No. This is rubbish. I'm going to make some more tea.

JOANNE. Yes, please!

She whispers in both their ears.

During the relative silence, we hear the doll.

DOLL. Mama! Mama!

They all stare at the doll, amazed.

JOANNE. That's the first time it's done that!

DOLL. Sorry. Little joke. Couldn't resist.

You're all under arrest. Resistance is futile. Put your hands behind your heads and leave the building. Resistance is futile.

The End.

A Nick Hern Book

The White Bike first published in Great Britain in 2017 as a paperback original by Nick Hern Books Limited, The Glasshouse, 49a Goldhawk Road, London W12 8QP, in association with Metal Rabbit and The Space Theatre, London

The White Bike copyright © 2017 Tamara von Werthern
The Village Church copyright © 2017 Tamara von Werthern
Baby Dolls copyright © 2017 Tamara von Werthern

Tamara von Werthern has asserted her moral right to be identified as the author of these works

Cover image: © Lily McLeish

Designed and typeset by Nick Hern Books, London
Printed in Great Britain by Mimeo Ltd, Huntingdon, Cambridgeshire PE29 6XX

A CIP catalogue record for this book is available from the British Library

ISBN   978 1 84842 683 2

www.nickhernbooks.co.uk

facebook.com/nickhernbooks

twitter.com/nickhernbooks